Günther Kunstmann

Acts 29

Signs and wonders -
they are still happening today!

A motivating book of facts

Günther Kunstmann

Acts 29

Signs and wonders - they are still happening today!

The exciting journey into the dimension of God

Reports about the works of Jesus today

A motivating book of facts

Bibliographic information of the German national library:
Published in the German national library;
detailed bibliographical data are retrievable on the internet over
http://dnb.dnb.de.

If not indicated differently, all the Biblical quotes are taken
from the New Living Translation.
Printed in bold type or notes in brackets
are an emphasis of the author.

© 2015 Günther Kunstmann, Bamberg/Germany

Title of the original version:
"Apostelgeschichte 29"
Translation into English:
Maria Deutsch / Bamberg / Germany
Editorial office: Helen Dresel / Sambach / Germany

Cover photography: © Günther Kunstmann

Publisher: Andra Kunstmann, Bamberg/Germany

Manufacturing and publishing company:
BOD – Books on Demand
Norderstedt/Germany

ISBN: 9783741250552

Dedication

I dedicate this book to the three people, who have affected my life with Jesus the most: my parents and my wife Andra!

To my parents
They have given me a safe and happy childhood and introduced me to Jesus and faith early on. Because of them I got to know Jesus and the Word of God and I learned to love it.

They encouraged me again and again to go on with Jesus in his way. To still believe, even if I could not understand some things yet or did not know how to put them into practice.

Their own life became an example to me in so many areas. During my years as a child and a youth, they always tried to put blessings into my life and a healthy awareness of the fact that Jesus loves me, that HE is always there for me and that my life has an importance and a calling. This awareness already showed up in an early class test, which I finished with the words:
"Through grace I am what I am."

It is such a huge present of God to have You as my parents.
Thank You very much for everything You have invested into my life.
Thanks for all the prayers, advice, support, warnings and tears for me and because of me.

The Lord Jesus, our mutual savior, richly bless you and offer you a lot more happy years. Your reward in heaven will be big.

Thank You very much, I love You!

To Andra,
the love of my life!

God brought us together, so that we would go through life together, grow with each other and with HIM. To discover faith in previously unknown dimensions, to serve God and the people and to win a lot of souls for Jesus, setting them on fire for HIM.

Thank you for your patience and support, when I did not understand some things, did not want to understand or rushed ahead.
Thanks for all your prayers that accompanied me in my job as a policeman, during my daily life and my spiritual ministry. Thank you for more than 34 years of marriage now with increasing love and joy for each other.

Thanks for all our journeys and adventures with Jesus,
I know it was not always easy for you with me.

You are a wonderful woman: strong, direct, a visionary and with strengthening faith.

Thank you for encouragement and support for this, my very first book. Somehow I have the suspicion that it will not be the last one.

My darling – I love you from the bottom of my heart!

Preface

In this book I will tell you something about my life. Just a normal life.
It is not a theological study or classical teaching book, but a personal testimony.
For that reason, I tell it as I have experienced it.

I will tell you how God managed to make me an active co-worker by his side. There were obstacles and blockages, but more and more victories became visible, as well.

I will tell you how I personally experienced healing, and how my wife and I got to pray for people worldwide, with amazing results.

Today we experience more and more miracles in the area of healing and God stepping in, so we want to spread this all around and explain it to the people for God to be honored.

All the reports told in this book have been personally experienced by us. We just left out the names for the people's privacy. That is why we only mention the gender and possibly the age at the time of healing.

If no other locations are mentioned, all the healings and incidents happened in the Jesus Gemeinde, Bamberg/Germany.

Under the headline "Report", Andra and I will tell you about the healing and miracles we experienced without mentioning unnecessary details.

When the word "Pastor" (or "wife of the Pastor") is used in a report, it is talking about my wife and me as the Pastors and leaders of the Jesus Gemeinde Bamberg.

Individual's reports are told from the first-person-perspective, because they were described like that to us.

I am writing this book because I am excited about Jesus again and again. And also about the things Jesus is still doing today, because I recognized that we don't get to hear about them often enough.

I am writing it because I am thankful that Jesus has lead me into the dimension of supernatural works. The things I had thought to be impossible years ago, are happening more and more in our life and through our ministry now.

To Jesus be all thanks and all honor! It is about HIM, not about me. Jesus is the savior, healer and the rescuer, not I.
I can and want to display his great works and his wonders.

We show the people who do not know Jesus yet, that HE loves them, that he is interested in them and also demonstrates that. We want to help them to come into a relationship with Jesus, setting them free, so that they can receive forgiveness and that their lives will get new meaning, help and strength. A life for eternity. A life here on earth with the possibility of experiencing this help and supernatural power themselves and also to give it to others.

I tell you: Jesus is so amazing; it will blow you away!

We want to encourage and challenge Christians to reflect on the conviction of their faith by means of the Bible and to ask and allow the Holy Spirit to lead them into new dimensions.

So that they are or become followers of Jesus who touch their surrounding with the Word of God and his power, who do signs and wonders to honor the heavenly Father, the almighty God, and to represent HIM in a way that is worth of HIM.

**Because that is
what you and I
are born for
and called to!**

Let's go
Auf geht's – Pack mer's
Vamonos

Günther and Andra Kunstmann
Bamberg, 2015

Table of contents

Dedication	5
Preface	7
It all started with hay fever	11
The sun will not harm you by day	27
Healing report Part I	39
"Prayer for healing"?	45
Healing report Part II	51
Demons flee	59
Reports of liberation	63
Unknown and silence	69
Healing report Part III	75
The Great Commission	83
Healing report Part IV	89
Amazing development	101
Do you know Jesus?	107
And everything comes different at once	113
Epilogue	129

It all started with hay fever

A dreadful discovery

You are around 30 years old, are thankful and happy that you have a strong, physical condition, you are making plans, you are ready to conquer the world and strong enough to pull out trees.
Who or whatever should be able to stop you?
And then my view of the world like this was completely turned upside down because of one incident:

Hay fever because of the grass pollen season!

The realization of this hit me like a ton of bricks, because I could not explain where it suddenly came from. I had never had an allergy before, I loved the scent of grass and hay, helped when the hay was reaped and I was feeling really good doing that. For me personally, spring time was one of the most beautiful times of the year.

Suddenly everything was different!
Burning, itching, swollen eyes; a scratching throat; a nose that kept running like a waterfall and no chance of healing. Medicine could only relieve it a bit.
So welcome to the club of the allergy sufferer!

This was a shattering prediction for my future.

Every year the time of the grass pollen season was horrific for me.
14 days' sick, spending time in a dark bedroom with the windows closed, eyes covered with Chamomile wet wipes – yeah great!)

Yearning for the pollen season to be over, so I could go out again. Into nature, back to my job, activities, friends and outings.

The mood at home with my wife was quite strained, tense, irritable during these 14 days – not what I had thought of as spring time.

You can surely imagine that in my head my thoughts were spinning around like in a merry-go-round. I knew plenty of people with various allergies and that they did not manage to get free from it, but had to get used to it their whole life.

Sometimes it was so bad that I wanted to live at the North Pole because the grass pollen didn't exist there. But then I realized that except for ice and snow nothing else existed there either! And so even that was no real alternative.

During this "time of suffering" this terrifying future was painted as clear as possible into my thoughts. I could twist and turn it, I did not see another solution other than to ask God to help me.

I knew: if anybody had a solution for my problem, then it was HIM!

"God is good" - uhm, excuse me?

As a child I grew up in a family with parents who frequently and joyfully went to a protestant independent church, and who loved Jesus Christ, God the Father and the Word of God with all their hearts. I went with them since my earliest childhood, it was absolutely normal for me to go to church and I happily grew up with it.

In early years (at the age of 13) I gave my life to Jesus. So prayers, promises of God and answered prayers were not strange to me. The church and faith were my usual surrounding. The Word of God gave me power and direction, especially during puberty. Till this day I am thankful to my parents, my brothers and sisters in faith and the church at that time for having taught me the "way of the LORD" and to have accompanied me. It helped me go through life quite stable.

Nevertheless, my way was not always straight and in my life I had done plenty of wrong things that made repentance, turning back and forgiveness necessary. Thank God, HE always forgave me and most of the people did too.

It was crystal-clear to me that God could heal.
Logical – HE was God and not just anyone. My conviction was that HE could do and not do whatever HE wanted to. Still, HE would be just in all these things. At least, that was a bit of consolation. This was how I had been taught. Of course I was praying for healing very intensively but it hardly changed anything. I thought "Well, then you will probably have to settle for that, maybe God does not want to heal you. Only others. It will be good for something somehow."

But I did not know for what it would be good for and I realized, that deep inside of me there was already a kind of inquiry to God - "and YOU are a good God?"

I did not want to question God but this little voice inside of me was not silenced.

This made me run into trouble because on the one hand I absolutely knew:
- God is good
- he loves me from the bottom of his heart
- he has good plans and intentions for my life
- I can always trust HIM
- he has given his son Jesus for me to be rescued
- the Bible is full of healing wonders and promises
- HE is almighty and very often we cannot understand him just with our brain
- the Word of God is for me and it is very practical
- …

but on the other hand I did not understand God and I wondered,
- what about the whole thing
- why me (I mean, I was his child)
- I was trusting HIM
- what did HE want to show or teach me by that
- why his Word did not work when I was praying
- and many more questions.

In the end I had to come to terms with it; I did it, had no solution, surrendered to my destiny – but I was not really happy with it.

An incredible realization

There are reports in the Bible you call the

Baptism into the Holy Spirit
or the
Infilling of the Holy Spirit

and which is available for all believers who have consciously invited and received Jesus as their Savior and Messiah and who live with HIM.
It does not come automatically but should be asked or prayed for!
So let's look at three scriptures.

*So if you sinful people know how to give good gifts
to your children, how much more will your heavenly Father
gives the Holy Spirit to those who ask him.*
Luke 11:13

*Then Peter and John laid their hands upon
these believers, and they received the Holy Spirit.*
Acts 8:15

*On the day of Pentecost all the believers were
meeting together in one place.
Suddenly, there was a sound from heaven
like the roaring of a mighty windstorm,
and it filled the house where
they were sitting.
Then, what looked like flames or tongues
of fire appeared and settled on each of them.
And everyone present was filled
with the Holy Spirit and
began speaking in other languages,
as the Holy Spirit gave them this ability.*
Acts 2:1-4

One day I got to receive this experience and it changed everything!

I will not explain how exactly I came to be baptized in the Holy Spirit - how it happened and what the first effects in my life were. That is another story that I may tell you at another point in time.

In any case, the infilling of the Holy Spirit always has to do something with new realizations too. Things you could not see or did not know before, are suddenly clear and understandable. It was the same with me.

> *When the Spirit of truth comes,*
> *he will guide you into all truth.*
> *He will not speak on his own but will tell you*
> *what he has heard. He will tell you about the future.*
> John 16:13

Suddenly I knew that the truths of the Word of God, the promises and statements about what Jesus has done and expensively bought at the cross for us – so also for me (!) - were available for me. Jesus had done it for me!
But I had no idea how to deal with that realization, let alone how to bring it into my life.

I started to pray and to ask Jesus to explain that to me, otherwise this realization would have been just for nothing! And HE did explain!

As an explanation I would like to mention that I did not start hearing voices or go into a trance somehow. But thoughts inside me recognized connections and understood what the Word of God expresses with certain scriptures, what it really means.

Sometimes there were these sudden thoughts I was wondering about, like "So where does this come from at once?"
Or it was like a dialogue on the inside. Very often it almost felt like suddenly I was right beside Jesus in a biblical report, experiencing everything as close as possible.
These thoughts and perceptions were connected with a big excitement, joy and expectation. Suddenly I knew what it meant to talk to God and also to get a reply.

I mean, I do know myself so I also know what and how I think. This kind of dialogue and these thoughts were new to me and were absolutely great. I knew this was God talking with me and inside me.

The infilling of the Holy Spirit had not really been taught in my church of the time. Speaking in other tongues, power effects, signs and wonders were known from the Bible (of course – it's written there in black and white) but there were plenty of people explaining why all these things were not for today or why it was not necessary. But there was also the occasional person I knew who had already had this experience with the Holy Spirit but they still seemed "exotic" in my eyes and a bit suspect.

So this experience with the Holy Spirit was the beginning of my journey in faith with Jesus, full of adventures, and it has changed my whole life.

First Steps

The first thing, God made clear to me, was as simple as:

"Have faith in my word and its power will be released!"

I said to HIM: "Since my earliest childhood I believed your word and have known a lot about it."
HE replied (in the described way): "Yes, you know a lot, still you do not really believe in most of the things but just say yes to everything. You think this is faith but it is not. Faith or to believe means trusting in the One, who once said it and act like it has already happened."

This was like a cold shower for me. And the same moment I knew: "HE is right!"

In a lot of situations, I did not act like God's Word wanted me to, I was a "Reichsbedenkenträger" (German, impossible to translate: a person who always doubts everything), I was searching for reasons in his word, that justified my behavior or doing nothing. I liked to take on so called faith statements such as "that's not for today" or "you can't know what God will do, you can't expect that from God" or "come on, you can't tell God what to do!", "better not get too extreme" and much more. Or I just had not got anything.

This new realization really put me in a fix. The only possible way was to commit that to Jesus and to ask him what to do.

Jesus showed me some scriptures in the Bible, which deal with "speaking" and the understanding of authority in faith.

Okay – the understanding of authority was not strange to me because of my job as a policeman and my experiences there.

When I was wearing my uniform and gave a signal to a heavy truck to stop, he stopped. Not because I am really big or frightening, not because I'm pretty or whatever, he stopped just because he has learned to respect signs of authority. (uhm – normally!) For example, he sees my uniform, my police hat, my police car etc.

There is even a scripture describing that.

> *When Jesus returned to Capernaum,*
> *a Roman officer came and pleaded*
> *with him, "Lord, my young servant lies in bed,*
> *paralyzed and in terrible pain.".*
> *Jesus said" I will come and heal him.".*
> *But the officer said, "Lord, I am not worthy*
> *to have you come into my house.*
> *Just say the word from where you are,*
> *and my servant will be healed.*
> *I know this because I am under*
> *the authority of my superior officers,*
> *and I have authority over my soldiers.*
> *I only need to say, 'Go,' and they go, or*
> *'Come,' and they come.*
> *And if I say to my slaves, 'Do this,' they do it."*
> *When Jesus heard this, he was amazed.*
> *Turning to those who were following him,*
> *he said, "I tell you the truth,*
> *I haven't seen faith like this in all Israel!"*
> Matthew 8:5-10

> Then Jesus said to the Roman officer, "Go back home.
> Because you believed,
> it has happened."
> And the young servant was healed that same hour.
> Matthew 8:13

Wow – I understood that. Suddenly I found more scriptures and got the connection.

> After leaving the synagogue that day,
> Jesus went to Simon's home,
> where he found Simon's mother-in-law
> very sick with a high fever.
> "Please heal her," everyone begged.
> Standing at her bedside,
> he rebuked the fever, and it left her.
> And she got up at once and prepared a meal for them.
> Luke 4:38-39

> I tell you the truth, you can say to this mountain,
> 'May you be lifted up and thrown into the sea,'
> and it will happen. But you must
> really believe it will happen
> and have no doubt in your heart.
> Mark 11:23

That gave me the last push! I knew what I had to do now:

> The hay fever was my mountain!
> I had to speak to it in authority!!
> I could believe it because my Father in heaven
> had said it and had let it be written!!!
> In faith I had the authority over this mountain!!!!
> I had to get up and get active!!!!!

Well then – action!

The time of the grass pollen came and with it my time of being tested. When the first signs of itching eyes tried to arise, I laid my hands onto my eyes and commanded:

"In Jesus name: hay fever, leave; itching, stop it!"

What do you think happened?
Immediately the itching left my eyes but started in my nose. I had never had something like that before.
It started running like a waterfall. I would not be discouraged, because I had just started and I am not the kind of person who likes to give up somewhere in between. So I went on. Perseverance and persistence were of paramount importance at that hour.
Again I laid my hands onto my nose and commanded:

"In Jesus' name: hay fever, leave; nose, stop itching and running!"

Promptly it stopped, but only to immediately appear in my throat.
The same game:

"Throat, stop itching; hay fever leave in the name of Jesus!"

It immediately stopped.

Whoever thinks, that was it, is wrong here. I was not the hero in faith I had imagined or expected. Winning – you must be joking. After only one round!
The whole thing started again just like at the beginning. The eyes were itching and watering – once again I laid my hands on it and commanded in the name of Jesus. Again this change to the nose – throat – eyes – nose and so on.

I would not give up, but full of trust I put the Word of God against it. Suddenly I had the impression like this here was a form of "spiritual arm wrestling". Well, arm wrestling was something I had always been good at.

So this went on for about an hour. Thank God, nobody had seen me doing that, I was alone at home. I felt absolutely freaky now. But what can I tell you?

After that very hour there was calm for the rest of the day. The hay fever had withdrawn, offended and beaten, but only to come back stronger the next day. It had probably brought some buddies with it.

But I had also become stronger in faith, so the "arm wrestling" was went on. The times of confrontation, which means the symptoms, got shorter and shorter. The victory came faster than the day before.

It went on for about one week, then the hay fever was gone.

I had never experienced something like that before. Hallelujah! What a feeling! Like I was floating on clouds.

I had perceived that this was about a spiritual dimension, with visible effects on my life. Suddenly I realized that there was much more behind things than I had been aware.

I suddenly understood the Bible to be a God-given tool, calling things into existence or working against them.

The test

So I got back to work – fresh, devout, happy and without any problems. During my absence my colleagues had discussed what to do for our work outing. One of them had had the bright idea to take a bike ride through our beautiful region. There were one or two alternatives. When I was back again, proposals for the outing were made and after it, a vote was taken. Incredibly fast the alternatives did not find agreement, and everyone voted for the bike ride.
Everyone? No – there was one vote against it. I will give you three guesses who it was from.

So, bike ride. Democratic decision by the majority. I did not tell anybody why exactly I was against it. I did not want to be a spoilsport to the others and secretly I thought "So just stay at home, you do not have to do that to yourself".

The day was coming closer and closer and of course I did not tell anyone of my secret plans. But somehow Jesus had noticed and HE spoke to me about them.
"Have you not successfully fought against the hay fever? Why do you not go along?"

Very quickly I had a good answer: "I don't want to strain my immune system too much now after this glorious battle, it has to relax a bit. In addition, you don't have to challenge things like that."
I felt pretty smart and thought it looked good to argue with God with a scripture. So at least HE could see that I knew something. That's why I added: "Even your Word tells us not to test God, as well."

That was a good point. Even HE could not oppose anything against this argument.
I felt good and had done everything right.

That's what I thought.
In fact, Jesus did not add anything.

The next time I opened up my Bible this one verse seemed to attack at me like a hungry lion:

> *Just as the body is dead without spirit,*
> *so also faith is dead without good works.*
> James 2:26

BINGO! Once again, Jesus had caught me. Immediately I knew what HE wanted to say and what it meant to me. Actually really clearly and simply. And I had thought I would have a trick up my sleeve.
Through this word HE made clear to me that faith is proved in practice. Now I had to get active, showing the others where I was standing, what I believed and that I had really won.

The others were:
- myself
- the people who knew about it
- God
- the devil, who had caused the problem for me
- and last but not least - the hay fever.

Now I had to show that faith is not only theoretical or theological knowledge. I had to prove that today faith in the Word of God still works just like in the time of Jesus and even before, an active, practical faith with visible, positive results.

The bike torture

So let's go on the bike ride. Greatest weather, Grass as far as the eye could see. The hay harvest on the fields was in full swing, big machines were whirling the dry grass around, so it was the whole deal.
And to me it seemed like all the grass pollen in the whole area had only one aim: my mucous membranes!
Mamma Mia! This was not just a bike tour – it was a bike torture!

But nevertheless I could feel the Holy Spirit right beside me, encouraging and motivating me. So the whole day I was fighting in my thoughts or, when nobody noticed, also very quietly, with the scriptures God had given to me that day.

Yet it was our sicknesses he carried;
it was our diseases that weighed him down.
And we thought his troubles were a punishment from God,
a punishment for his own sins!
But he was pierced for our rebellion,
crushed for our sins. He was beaten so we could be whole.
He was whipped so we could be healed.
Isaiah 53:4-5

Put on salvation as your helmet,
and take the sword of the Spirit, which is the word of God.
Ephesians 6:17

The Holy Spirit made these words come alive for me and I felt the power and the truth of these verses. In addition, HE said to me "Take these sentences personally, pronounce them by using the first-person-perspective. That is your sword against this attack.".

So I was quoting the famous scriptures of Isaiah 53 and Ephesians 6 in this perspective:

Yet it was MY sicknesses he carried;
it was MY diseases that weighed him down.
And I thought his troubles were a punishment from God,
a punishment for his own sins!
But he was pierced for MY rebellion,
crushed for MY sins. He was beaten so I could be whole.
He was whipped so I could be healed.
Isaiah 53:4-5

I put on salvation as MY helmet,
and take MY sword of the Spirit, which is the word of God.
Ephesians 6:17

My eyes were itching; the pollen were tickling my nose … but they had no chance.
I kept on solidly with the Word of God.
When I was driving home this very evening, I knew deep inside me: It is done!
Also externally the victory was visible: not a single symptom anymore! Glory to God!

Since that time – now it is more than 30 years (!) ago - the hay fever has never ever returned again.

I can only say:

WOW -
Thank You, Jesus!
All honor to You!

The sun will not harm you by day

Ski holidays – I like it

I would like to tell you one more story to show you how powerful the Word of God is and this story encouraged me in an incredible way and made me learn more.

Before that I want to explain two biblical terms that are important for understanding.
It is about "logos" and "rhema".
As this is no teaching book but one that shares personal experiences of adventures with God and challenges that could be victoriously won with the help of the Holy Spirit, I will make it quite short.
For me, the Greek word "logos" is about the Word of God in general. The whole Bible. You can read it just like a normal book or a magazine, and you will experience nothing. Or you read it as the Word of God; it is the truth and you are entitled to take it for yourself.

The word "rhema" means to me:
- a special word from God
- for a special time
- for a special situation
- stressed by the Holy Spirit.

There are situations when God gives us a special word to be able to master a situation. Remember the bike ride – I got two special verses to defend myself against the renewed hay fever attack and to defeat this allergy completely. That was a "rhema".
There are a lot of good books about it so I do not need to write another one.

With friends, Andra and I went for skiing holidays in Austria. To Sölden in the Ötztal. We wanted to go skiing in Hochsölden where the ski resort is over 3300 meters high.
Fantastic weather: blue sky, sun shining brightly, picture-book snow
Dear – what more could you want?

Of course, with sun lotion on my face - not too much and not with a too high a sun protection factor. I mean, you want to get a tan. Up to the ski-run and enjoying the day. As much as possible. The whole day.
Finally, the evening came and with it - the sunburn.
Sunburn to the maximum!
My whole face was scarlet, burning like fire and covered in blisters. I couldn't even touch my skin.

Okay, bye bye to my skiing holiday! One day of fun and then total disaster.
The annoying thing was, we had already paid for the ski pass and the boarding house for one week.
The others were alright – for whatever reason.
I spent the whole evening putting on lotions and praying for a miracle of healing.
Nothing! No change. I was in pain and my face looked like a red balloon. Of course, I could not sleep at night because I did not know where to put my head.

It was a perfect disaster and I was helpless once again.

Der Morgen graute – mir auch!
(German wordplay, impossible to translate, like: Dawn was coming up and I was dreading it.)

I had no idea what I ought to do. I didn't want to spoil the skiing holiday for the others.
As I normally did, I spent my time before breakfast with praying and reading the Bible.
And in fact Jesus had come with us to the Ötztal to talk to me and to help me.

>"The sun will not harm you by day."

Suddenly this thought was there and it would not let me go. Again and again this sentence came up to my mind. Somehow I knew it but I could not place it. So I asked Jesus: "Where do I know this sentence from?"
He told me it was a Psalm I knew very well. Once I had written a song about it. And in my Bible I found the chords I had written down at the time.
Ah, well – that was where I knew it from. Jesus was right – as always.

To mention at this point, since my youth I had been playing the guitar passionately. In early years I started to write my own songs with Bible texts or about faith. And I still love doing it. Writing songs about how great Jesus is and the signs and wonders he is still doing today, or songs of worship.

I remembered that and I was searching for that Psalm, completely equipped with guitar chords, in my Bible. That was my search pattern. I was glad to have my little, old Bible translated by Martin Luther, which had been a present from my parents for my baptism in 1970. It accompanied me everywhere I went. Time after time I add notes to the scriptures in it.

Very lovely, my parents had written a dedication inside of it:

> "For our dear Günther, to be used as a blessing.
> Your parents
> in remembrance to your baptism,
> December 6, 1970"

And as it was written so it happened! Psalm 121 seemed to laugh at me.

G-major – E-minor – C-major – D-major.

> *I look up to the mountains –*
> *does my help come from there?*
> *My help comes from the LORD,*
> *who made heaven and earth!*
> *He will not let you stumble; the one who watches*
> *over you will not slumber.*
> *Indeed, he who watches over Israel*
> *never slumbers or sleeps.*
> *The LORD himself watches over you!*
> *The LORD stands beside you*
> *as your protective shade.*
> *The sun will not harm you by day,*
> *nor the moon at night.*
> *The LORD keeps you from all harm and watches*
> *over your life.*
> *The LORD keeps watch over you as you come and go,*
> *both now and forever.*
> Psalm 121

Bam! It was the absolute hit. An incredibly good skiing-Psalm. Eyes up to the mountains; HE will not let you stumble; HE keeps you from all harm.
So nothing bad could happen to me anymore. I had never seen this psalm in this way before.

And here it was, the sentence:

> *"The sun will not harm you by day,
> nor the moon at night."*

Okay, I did not care about the moon at night in that moment. But the words about the sun and its harm, was exactly for me. I quickly recognized that the writer of the Psalm wasn't actually talking about skiing.
Obviously – I mean, how, where or why?

So the secret of the Psalm had to lay elsewhere.
While I was thinking of that, the unmistakable, gentle voice of the LORD came into my thoughts.

> "This is your verse for your skiing today.
> Go with the others and hold up this word.
> The sun will not be able to harm you."

That was just about the limit. The sun would not be able to harm me. Enough to make a cat laugh. It had never been like that before.

But meanwhile I knew the voice of Jesus and I trusted it more than all laws of nature, biology or physics teachers or any other good opinions and advice. It was not that they were not important to me, but – well, the Word of God and the voice of the Holy Spirit are more important to me than them.

In addition, I had never forgotten my "battle against the hay fever". How could I ever forget that? It had been so exciting and successful.

Sun Lotion or the Word of God

So get ready to do parallel turns. The whole rig-out, face full of sun lotion, let's go …
Wait, not like this! I stopped and thought hard. If I lotion very well and in the evening everything is alright, I wouldn't know what exactly helped.

           The sun lotion or the Word of God.

I had to decide. Hop or top. Either – or. God or lotion. Victory or failure.

I ran back into my room; the others were already waiting for me at the car. I washed away the sun lotion with soap, careful to get everything off.
Okay – done.
Out of the mirror a scarlet face looked back at me and I knew it from somewhere. This face seemed to shout at me:

      So now you are completely crazy, right?
            You will burn hopelessly.
              This is irresponsible.
           You will end up in hospital.
                 Stay at home!

I hesitated. Suddenly the way I was acting seemed crazy to me. What should I do, time was running out. Very short, like in slow motion, a story from the Old Testament appeared to my inner eye.
Three men of God, who did not want to bow down before the wrong God, were punished by being thrown into a furnace.
You can read the whole fantastic story in the Old Testament, in the book of Daniel, chapter 3, from verse 1 to 30. I recommend it to you.

The sentence, which became important and a confirmation for me, was:

*If we are thrown into the blazing furnace,
the God whom we serve is able to save us.
He will rescue us from your power, Your Majesty.*
Daniel 3:17

The blazing furnace, that was it. I did know how the story would end. The fire could not harm the three guys because Jesus joined them and protected them.
It was like a confirmation for me.
So I said "adios" to the face in the mirror and jumped into our car.

Again another fantastic day of absolutely great weather. And one of the hardest days of my life.
Up to 3000 meters, closer to the sun and very close to the challenge.
My life almost literally depended on the Word of God.

My thoughts were racing. What, if you were wrong, if you were just imagining it?
Like a confirmation I felt the sun burning onto my face. The fight was getting started. The battle went wild. I was like a warrior standing between two armies.

The white army was encouraging me, saying:
- the Word of God is true
- keep to it
- do not let thoughts get you crazy
- not all of the other thoughts are wrong but the truth of God is more correct
- the victory is yours
- for those who believe, nothing is impossible
- ...

The black army attacked me:
- you are totally mad
- the laws of physics are forever and unchanging
- think of the consequences
- who do you think you are to challenge nature
- you will suffer terribly
- …

It went on like this for the whole day. But I was getting bolder and bolder and I was holding up the word I had got from God like an invisible sunshade. It was a similar confrontation like it had been with the hay fever only much fiercer.
I was calling at the sun: Hey, you know you are not allowed to harm me?! You are forbidden to do it by the Word of God!
I was pretty bold and maybe even a bit cheeky.

And everything up there at 3000 meters, with a lot of sun, UV light and reflection of snow.

The skiing day came to an end and I was quite shattered. But I was also at the end of the battle – as the winner. In the evening the others and I could establish that my face was no longer red and swollen but normal. The sun had not been able to harm me. On the contrary – despite of intensive sun rays my burnt face had healed during the day.
When I looked into the mirror that evening, I saw a familiar, happy, satisfied and glorious face and I told it:

> That's what winners look like – sleep well!

Once again, faith in Jesus and in his everlasting, powerful Word had won. It was an experience that would influence my whole life.

> *"Does not my word burn like fire?" says the LORD.*
> *"Is it not like a hammer that smashes a rock to pieces?"*
> Jeremiah 23:29

> *Heaven and earth will disappear,*
> *but my words will never disappear.*
> Mark 13:31

> *Your word is a lamp to guide my feet*
> *and a light for my path.*
> Psalm 119:105

The Word of God is absolutely true and trustworthy. It is powerful and mighty to overcome everything. It will last for all eternity. It will still stand in authority when all the words of clever humans, the words of any religious founders or others have already faded away. Why?
Because Jesus Himself is the Word of God.

You can theorize it, pick it apart, call it untrue, question it, complicate it or whatever. Nothing of its veracity will be changed.

I, for myself, have decided to fully trust in the Word of God, even though I do not understand everything yet and I cannot answer every single question. Even if people come to me with arguments that sound good and right but still are against the Word of God, I stick with the Word. My personal condition does not decide the truth of the Word of God.

Risks and side effects

I want to warn you here, not just to copy it because I experienced it like that.

> It was a clear Word of God,
> for a special time in a special situation
> **for me!**
> A clear rhema!
> (Not rheuma-tism! Do not mix it up!)

What's the saying??
"For risks and side effects, read your Bible or ask the Holy Spirit!"

You have to undergo your own experiences with Jesus, HE leads you in the steps of faith. And I promise you, you will experience victory and miracles. But please do not just copy anything.
It is my experience, my fights and victories and I am sharing them with you, so you know:

> Still today, the Word of God is valid and mighty.
> It is worth searching for more of Jesus.
> Be on the way, HE has already been waiting for You.
> Tell the adventure, you are coming.

Trust in Jesus and in his word. Start occupying yourself with the Word of God and read about the miracles Jesus and the disciples did and how they did them.

Contact other Christians who practice that and who have already experienced healing wonders themselves.
Please no chatterboxes who have heard about someone who knows somebody who has heard about a miracle. Or those who always have got answers for everything, but in whose lives no miracles and healings are happening.

It is a personal process of growing. But it is exciting and it is worth it. God does not have one special method but uncountable possibilities. God is not religious, he loves you and he wants to work together with you, considering your personality. After all, HE has given it to you.

The following reports of healing or other actions of God may
- surprise you
- amaze you
- get you enthusiastic
- confuse you
- inflame you
- motivate you.

Some happenings may seem to be little things to you but when you are in a situation like that, having pains or problems, it is big for you. And you are thankful when they leave.

The reports are for God to be honored and they show the works of Jesus in our time today. They show how I grew in faith, step by step, using my authority and the healing multiplied.
I told you at the beginning, either Andra or I, or the person themselves are telling you their report, as they experienced it. In that case, I have written it down in the first-person-perspective.

It can be recognized by the heading.

Fasten your seat belt – hold tight – let's go!

Here you can take some notes about what you have read so far, reflecting on it later.

Healing reports Part I

Goodbye shoulder pain -
healing from an aching shoulder sprain

A 16-year old pupil reports:
I had fallen onto my right shoulder in school. Since that fall I could hardly move it. It was terribly painful. The same day in the evening we had Bible school in the Jesus Gemeinde Bamberg and eventually I asked the Pastor to pray for my shoulder. I did not want to go to the doctor yet because I believed that Jesus would heal me.
After the prayer the pain had almost left, I could move my arm better. I was sent home with the encouragement to go on moving my arm, the pain would completely leave.

Jesus hadn't finished with it yet – but he would bring it to an end.

And in fact it was like this. Days later the Pastor asked me about it. The pain had totally left and the shoulder was as working as normal.

Eyes are there to see! -
God's goodness doesn't take age into account

A grandma (80 years old) reports:
I was working in the kitchen, when suddenly a veil came over my right eye and I could hardly see anything. I could only see a tiny bit of light.
The doctor, I was going to, said he was not able to do anything anymore, I had to settle for complete blindness in that eye.
I did not get discouraged because of the diagnosis, because I have been living with Jesus for many years of my life by then and I knew my savior. I confided in him, his kindness and grace and prayed for the healing of my eye.
Also in church the eye was prayed for and the blindness was commanded to leave in the name of Jesus.
During the following weeks, my eyesight in this eye improved step by step so I was even able to do the test at the doctors. The only thing I could not read was the very last, small line. But I knew that would be alright as well.

The veil on the eye left and has stayed gone till now.

I praise Jesus for that.

Crooked for 30 years! -
healing from lateral curvature of the spine

Another older, lovely lady:
30 years ago, when I was still working, one day I had to climb up a stool to take something out of the smoker. At the same time, I slipped off and hit the concrete floor laterally. After that I had incredible pain and during the next few months I noticed that my spine had moved, so that it was crooked. I could not do anything against it and had lived with it for 30 years.

During a Pentecostal service in church, the Holy Spirit was moving in a mighty way. The power of God came upon me and Jesus started shaking me. I was jumped up and down wildly and at first did not know what it was about. For a lady at my age, this is not a way to behave during a service, normally. But I knew it was Jesus, that is why I allowed it.

Following this I was surprised to notice that the lateral curvature of my spine was gone and I could stand straight again without any pain. It was a forgotten, but beautiful feeling to not stand crooked after 30 years.

I have experienced the healing power of God in a very unusual way and at a older age.

Thank God, age is no obstacle for Jesus to act.

Torn finger tendon healed! -
surgery unnecessary

A young woman tells us:
I had been attacked in my neighborhood by a drunken youth, so my hand was injured. I could not move my ring finger anymore. That is why I went to the doctor and after having examined it he detected that my tendon on my finger was ripped. It had to be operated on for the finger to not become stiff. Following that I had to wait for it until the enormous swelling had subsided. I had a cast on my hand.

In church, the pastor came up to me, asking what had happened. I told him everything and before the service he prayed with me and commanded the torn tendon to heal up again.

One week later – I was in the service again and the swelling had completely gone. The finger worked without any pain. The tendon was alright again, it left the doctor faced with a riddle.

Surgery was unnecessary because God had healed me.

Immune system gone crazy -
trying to repulse all the body muscles, the immune system fails against Jesus

Report:
On Sunday, 11th November 2012, a 47-year old man from our church was brought into hospital, as an emergency, in the early hours of the morning.
He could hardly move his body and was without any strength in his limbs. He could not even raise his foot on his own, let alone hold a glass of water or open a bottle.

The doctors caring for him found out that his immune system was in chaos. It was suddenly fighting against his muscles. All his muscles were inflamed and because of that he was in unbearable pain. The doctors did not know the reasons.

Sunday morning his wife told us his critical situation in the service. In the early afternoon, Andra and I were drove to the hospital to visit him. He confirmed the diagnosis of the doctors and that they had to wait for the latest examinations of the laboratory to try to find a possible treatment. But it would probably involve a strong cortisone treatment with an uncertainty concerning his future mobility.

So we laid our hands upon him, prayed for healing and commanded this sickness to leave in the name of Jesus. We proclaimed complete restoration and a normal functioning of the immune system.

After only about two minutes, strength came back to his limbs, so before our eyes he was able to hold a full bottle of mineral water again. He lifted his legs, bending them. Before prayer he had not been able to do that either.

Glory to God!

The pains decreased but he still was not that well. He improved over the next few hours.

One Sunday later, he joined the service again, and reported that the doctors had let him go because they could not find anything anymore.
The tests were absolutely normal. The doctors had no explanation for that.

Oh yes – and on Saturday he had already cut wood again. His strength had returned 100 %.

Jesus is so good and in HIS name there is power over the disease.

"Prayer for healing"?

Actually, prayer for healing is a command

Here I would like to explain something very important.
For better understanding, we are talking about prayer for healing. People can connect with that.

But actually, it is not a prayer for healing but a command.
Because prayer is talking to God and listening to him.
We do not pray for healing, but we speak and command the problems to leave because Jesus has told us to do so.
In this case, we do not command God (how could we?), but the "mountain"!

> *I tell you the truth, you can **say** to this mountain:*
> *'May you be lifted up and thrown into the sea,'*
> *and it will happen. But you must really believe*
> *it will happen and have no doubt in your heart.*
> Mark 11:23

> *But Peter **said**,*
> *"I don't have any silver or gold for you. But I'll give you what I have.*
> ***In the name of Jesus Christ of Nazareth,***
> ***get up and walk!***
> *Then Peter took the lame man by the right hand*
> *and helped him up.*
> *And as he did, the man's feet and ankles*
> *were instantly healed*
> *and strengthened. He jumped up,*
> *stood on his feet, and began to walk!*
> *Then, walking, leaping, and praising God,*
> *he went into the Temple with them.*
> Acts 3:6-8

There are many more scriptures, similar to that. Please notice, that it was not **prayed** for here. God in heaven was **not** begged to do anything.
Jesus said: If you have no doubt in your heart but believe it will really happen and **speak** to this mountain (= problems, disease …)!

Peter did **not** pray: "Oh, Jesus in heaven, I know you can heal him. Look at this poor guy. Have mercy with him and please heal him, if you want."

NO!!!!!!!

He spoke, forceful, enthusiastically and with firm conviction. He was aware of what Jesus had taught him. He knew the will of God. He had been there as an eyewitness of uncountable healing wonders and other miracles. There was no doubt in him.
He should do it this way.

He was not distracted or irritated by the question:
- Is it God's will?
- Are these my instructions for here and now?
- Is he still paralyzed because he has not learned the lesson that God wants to teach him?
- What if nothing happens?
- Won't we make a fool not only of ourselves but also of Jesus and in public?

I want to shortly explain that to you.

A question of authority

I have explained it in connection with the report about the hay fever story and the sunburn whilst skiing incident. It is then that I understood what the Word of God explains explicitly.

>I have authority from Jesus to act in His Name.

That means, I know what Jesus wants, what is available and what I'm allowed to or not allowed to do.
This is the understanding of authority and faith. Taking God at his Word because HE has said and also meant it like that.
I act as an authorized person, in the name and the power of the One who has given me the job to do so.

I want to illustrate it with my job as a policeman.
The state has taken me into its employment and has trained me to ensure that law and order is kept to the letter. It uses a lot of money and time to educate me well until it lets me go out on the streets. I get an ID card, that justifies and identifies me as an authorized person for others to respect the law. Everything I need is available for me. A uniform, weapon, police car, computer, paper, my salary and so on.

As long as I act as an authorized agent, the state will support me because it is my employer and it will also legally stand behind me and my actions. It protects me.

Everything all right to here.

A wrong understanding, however, would be if I called the Home Secretary just to ask him to please caution this new car driver who has parked his car in a no-parking zone.
The Home Secretary would answer (probably very enthusiastically): That's your job, that's why I have authorized you.

With faith it is the same.
Jesus has authorized us to do things in His Name. Speaking to problems and diseases in order to change them.

Here there are two pieces of biblical evidence.

> *The Lord now chose seventy-two other disciples and*
> *sent them ahead in pairs to all the towns*
> *and places he planned to visit ...*
> *(and gave them the job and authorized them)*
> *... Heal the sick and tell them,*
> *'The Kingdom of God is near you now'.*
> Luke 10:1+9

> *Look, I have given you authority over all the power*
> *of the enemy, and you can walk among snakes*
> *and scorpions and crush them.*
> *Nothing will injure you.*
> Luke 10:19

And the disciples did exactly that.
- they had received the order
- they had got the authority
- they should act in the Name of Jesus
- they had been given power
- and it worked!

The more I occupy myself with it, understand it and put it into practice, the more things happen. I see a ever-increasing number of healing wonders and miracles in my life.

It is the same with my wife.

Very often other Christians confront us saying that they don't understand it like that and – does everyone get healed? What about those who have not been healed?
Mostly, our reply is quite simple.

We can see it like that because so does Jesus.

and

**At the moment, not everybody is getting healed but more and more are.
Better to have one healed than to have none at all.**

What is the use of having a high theological discussion with a person who is in pain? It cannot bring any relief or healing. Jesus had the same conflict with the Pharisees and the teachers of the religious law of his time. His response to them was distinct – very distinct. Jesus left them standing, turned around and healed and set the people free.

There are a lot of books, say that there are no more miracles today, that we do not need the powerful works of the Holy Spirit, that not every Christian is called to that and many more arguments.
I have no idea how these people came upon that.

For me personally, these kind of books are not worth the paper they are printed on.

That is why an amazing report of our missionary journey to Argentina is about to be described.

Put your seat belt on – keep tight – let's go on:

Here you can take some notes about what you have read so far, reflecting on it later.

Healing reports Part II

Paraplegia healed -
young wheelchair user jumping around again and a lot of more healing wonders

Report:
In April 2012, Andra and I were on a preaching journey in La Plata, Argentina. On Sunday, 29th April 2012, I was preaching in Club Atenas, a big gymnasium, in which the church "Un Estilo de Vida" meets for their service. Their own church rooms could not take the 2500 or so church members (at that time) any longer, and each week their number was increasing.

I was preaching about Jesus, how HE had already met people and how HE had healed them. During the preaching I was demonstrating that with various people and they were immediately healed. Suddenly I was standing in front of a young wheelchair user, about 16 or 18 years old.

Mamma mia! What to do now? My thoughts were racing. A wheelchair user of all people and about 2000 people expectantly looking at me.
Help! God! - couldn't it have been a person with headache? But faith means acting and trusting. So grit your teeth and get to it.

Through the microphone – so everyone could hear it – I asked him what his problem was and he told me that he had been member of a "street gang" and that he had been involved in a shooting. So he had got five bullets in his spine, which was inoperable and still stuck inside.
From the hips down he was paraplegic. He had no feeling in his legs and was not able to move them even a millimeter.

Jesus gave me a word from the Book of Acts, where Peter

and John heal the paralyzed man at the "Beautiful Gate" of the Temple. They gave him their hand and pulled him up in the Name of Jesus. You can read it yourself, if you want, in the book of Acts, chapter 3, from verses 1 to 25.

Boldly, I did the same and nothing happened. With two helpers I pulled the young man out of the wheelchair and we put him up on his feet, but he could not stand on his own. We dragged him for a few steps but then had to let him sit in the wheelchair again for there was no reaction in his legs. He was beaming from ear to ear.

I received a prophetic word from Jesus for him, that when we returned next year, I would run with him through the Club Atenas. He was still beaming at me, although he obviously had not received healing.

I thought, okay – let's see.

I called the people to give their lives to Jesus and to entrust it to HIM. Jesus wanted to save people now, to forgive their sins and to offer them eternal life. I was pretty surprised when at this altar call the young wheelchair user came to the front and beaming he gave his life to Jesus.

Hallelujah – this is worth more than any healing.

> *In the same way, there is more joy in heaven*
> *over one lost sinner who repents and returns to God*
> *than over ninety-nine others who are righteous*
> *and haven't strayed away!*
> Luke 15:7

Two days later we flew to Brazil. An e-mail from La Plata reached us one week later, in which we were told that on Sunday, the young wheelchair user had been in the service again.
He had openly given a report about that he had felt his legs again, the week after we had prayed for him, and that he could already move his right leg a bit.
There was great rejoicing in the whole church.

For the rest of the year, I did not hear anything more from this boy.
When in November 2012 the pastor of this church, Raul Reyes, came to our conference "Come Holy Spirit" in Bamberg, we had a conversation about the boy and I asked how he was now. Pastor Raul said that of course the boy could walk again and he frequently visited the church. He was completely restored. They had just forgotten to give us the information.

This time there was great rejoicing in our church. God had not only saved the boy but also totally healed him.

One year later we were in La Plata again in a service in Club Atenas. I was looking forward to meeting the young man. I remembered my promise and I was prepared. I wanted to interview him and to record it on video because it was so incredible. So I asked where he was in the huge crowd of people and that he should come to the front. I could not remember his face, let alone his name. So I openly called him to the public. Nobody came.

A young man piped up, said he was a friend of the healed one. Unfortunately, he was not there that day, he was away somewhere and had not remembered this service. But he was alright, running around and going to church.
'What a pity,' I thought, 'today of all days he is not there.' I had been looking forward to it so much.

But isn't Jesus great? Five bullets in the spine do not really matter to HIM.

To Jesus be all thanks and honor for this enormous miracle.

More miracles

During our preaching journey in Argentina and Brazil, a lot of more people got healed. We were preaching the Kingdom of God and HIS love and grace. The Holy Spirit lead us into the direction of preaching the Kingdom of God and his power and demonstrating that. Each time we did it, people got healed. For Andra and me it was a new level of authority and a previously unknown easiness for healing wonders. A lot of salvation and liberation for people was taking place.

Kidney stones dissolved
We had been invited to a birthday party. Among the numerous guests there also was an older man who could neither sit nor stand because of pain. He had come, but after a while he was doubled up with pain, sweating from his whole face. The reason was, he told us, the presence of large kidney stones that had been diagnosed.
In Jesus' name I commanded them to dissolve.
A few minutes later he went to the bathroom and during urination he could see how the dissolved kidney stones were washed out. He could hear it rattle in the toilet.
After that he had no more pain and he celebrated with us enthusiastically.

Pains disappear after years
For years, a woman had had violent pains in her whole body and none of the doctors she had went to could find a reason for them, let alone a solution. After prayer she fell to the ground under the power of God. When she came up again after some time and I asked her how she felt, she said she felt "spectacular". Even some days later there was no more pain and she could sleep well again.

Bent hands working again
An older woman had arthritis in her hands so much so that she could not open her bent fingers anymore. The whole church knew the woman and helped her with her daily work because she could not do it anymore. Specifically, I spoke to this arthritis and commanded to immediately leave the woman in the Name of Jesus. The very same moment she got healed and could demonstrate it to the church. She held her hands up, stretching her fingers and moving them wildly.

Never ending healing wonders
Damaged knees, various pains, arthritis in wrists / ankles and shoulder / neck, twisted spines, slipped disks and many many more things were healed during the five weeks of our journey in the services. It was exciting to see what Jesus did.

You know, when somebody tells me that there are no more miracles like that today, I think - I'm in a different movie!

Every day it is happening all around the world, also here in Germany and Bamberg. Wherever all kinds of Christians start praying in the power of the Holy Spirit and in the Name of Jesus, salvation, healing, liberation and other miracles happen.

These things are totally normal – or they should be.

Hives healed / bones grown! -
Incurable healed nevertheless

A middle-aged woman told us:
For years I had had hives. They were very painful and really annoying. I looked like I had been whipped. All my skin was covered with welts and felt like there beetles eating beneath them. It itched madly, so very often I scratched myself so much it bled. The doctor said I had to live with it, hives were incurable and only little researched. To help relieve it I got a strong corticosteroid ointment.

In one of the previous services I had prayer and since that very day the hives left. My doctor cannot understand it at all.

I also had another problem. Because of an extensive surgery on my thigh, my bone had been sawn apart so that 2 centimeters of my bone was missing. I had one leg too short with all the side effects that has, like pain in the back, the lumbar region and so on. To level out the difference I had to wear a shoe sole increase in the one shoe.

After a sermon about the believers' authority, a woman from church prayed with me in the service. She immediately put what she had heard into practice and commanded the bone to grow – and at that same moment it did!
Now I have got two legs that have the same length again, so I don't need height-adjusting insoles anymore.

To God be all honor. What is impossible for men, is possible for God.

The end of an alcoholic -
Jesus sets free!

A man's report (43 years):
I grew up in the former USSR and having studied music was working in a hard rock band, of course also playing at any every other event. I was earning quite a lot with that job and there was always plenty of alcohol. I was married, had two children and everything was fine until I recognized that I was drinking more and more alcohol because we had enough of it. Affairs, excesses and especially the alcohol eventually caused me become an alcoholic. My marriage broke apart and everything went down the tubes.

Finally, I moved to Germany with my mom and my brother, I got a flat and a job as a factory worker. But still the alcohol did not let me go. Meanwhile I was divorced and the children stayed with my ex-wife.

Through friends I got to know Jesus - they told me he was the Son of God and he wanted to forgive me my sins. I decided to give my broken life into the hand of Jesus, prayed for forgiveness and asked Jesus to set me free from alcohol.

In the meantime, I was also going to church where I met praying people who supported me and showed me that despite my addiction I was precious to Jesus. They always encouraged me to not give up, that Jesus would help me.

There was still one quite dramatic incident that made me notice that my life was insecure and unsettled. It was the final turning point. Was it to be death due to alcohol or living and being set free through Jesus. I had to choose whether to give up my life or to fully trust in God.
In the middle of the night, about at midnight, I experienced a horrific experience. It was dreadful. I saw and felt the

demons, mocking me and telling me they would kill me.

I cried out for Jesus and suddenly had the impulse, "Call your pastor!". Great, after midnight. I knew that my Pastor had an answering machine in his office and that he would probably not answer the phone. Nevertheless, I called him, hoping to reach him somehow.
And the unbelievable happened. He did answer the phone, quickly listened to my story and was with me only 15 minutes later. He prayed with me and commanded this demon of alcohol to leave my life. I could feel something dark, evil leaving my body and mind.

That is a few years ago now and I am still free today, my life has completely changed.
Without any withdrawal treatment or without physical withdrawal symptoms, Jesus set me free.

My life belongs to him and everywhere I get the chance to, I tell people about his liberating and restoring power.
The alcoholic inside of me is dead, but Jesus made me alive.

Demons flee

Jesus is stronger than the demons

Among others, the instructions Jesus gave to his disciples, were:
> "heal the sick, cast out demons."

Well, both of these go together.
According to the Bible, demons are evil spirits subordinate to the devil, with the job of keeping people away from Jesus and destroying their lives.

Jesus beat them through his death on the cross, he stripped them of all their power and he publicly put them on display.

> *In this way, he stripped off the spiritual rulers*
> *and authorities. He shamed them publicly*
> *by his victory over them on the cross.*
> Colossians 2:15

Here the apostle Paul, who has written that verse, refers to a usual custom of the Romans. After a victorious battle the Roman commander moved into the city in a triumphal procession. Behind him, the defeated enemies had to follow in chains. First the defeated king and his previously mighty subjected ones – naked! Each sign of power and worth and sublimity had been taken away from them and they were humbled in this way.
They were publicly put on display like circus monkeys. That was how the people were shown who the mightier king was and that the power and authority of the other one had been ended.

It was a public festival and a triumphal procession. Mostly, the people threw refuse, excrement and other unpleasant things at the defeated enemies.

Paul takes this picture to make clear what happened through Jesus at the cross. It was a triumphal procession over Satan and his henchmen. Jesus presents them to demonstrate that the devil's power has been ended.

That is why followers of Jesus Christ can take their authority over the demons and these have to – yeah, have to obey. The power of Jesus is so much greater than Satan's one. He is defeated. Hallelujah!

This triumphal procession is a very interesting and motivating thing to remember when we get in contact with "powers of the devil".

To be mentioned here - not everyone plagued by the devil is automatically possessed by him. When you hear about a topic like this, you immediately think of movies such as "The Exorcist" or "Rosemarie's Baby" and other horror movies.

A dirty coat

In my opinion, someone is possessed when he/she does not have any control over him-/herself anymore but is really externally controlled. Also here the power of Jesus is always stronger and victorious.
Most of the people who have to do something with demons suffer under the negative influences of them, shown in addictions, behavior or similar effects. But normally people are still masters of their minds.

I like to compare these influences with a dirty coat, put around humans by the demons. This dirty coat is the basis for their destructive activities. Due to the command in Jesus' Name, possibly repentance about sins connected with it and changed sustained behavior, the demons have to bow down and to leave together with their dirty coat.

This stinking coat and its demons come upon the lives of persons who occupy themselves with wrong things and open their souls for them. Starting with dealing with occult rituals, horror movies, certain music or literature, to inconspicuous daily things. Like only reading the horoscopes for fun because you allegedly do not believe in them anyway.
Lying, stealing, cheating and much more opens up the doors of your soul and your life for negative powers to come in.
Drugs, in particular, cause an easy entrance because they directly attack the psyche and so many times I have seen in other people, that even after a low consumption there are effects.

Today's society neglects the existence of demons, searching for biological/psychological explanations. Somethings might be explainable and curable but still many things are not.

The more society departs from God and from his Word, the more psychological sicknesses and disastrous conditions increase in the peoples' lives and in society. That should make us thoughtful. It is also striking that there are more and more movies with demonic scenes and themes even though these powers do not exist in their opinion. In the Catholic Church there is even the topic of exorcism, which is still practiced in a lot of countries today.

The real ghost-busters

So it is not surprising that Jesus gave authority to his disciples to cast these demons out of peoples' lives (because they do not leave voluntarily) and – it worked.

> *One day Jesus called the twelve apostles*
> *and gave them power and authority to cast out* ***all demons***
> *and to heal all diseases.*
> *Then he sent them out to tell everyone*
> *about the Kingdom of God*
> *and to heal the sick.*
> Luke 9:1+2

Jesus did the same with 72 other followers of him:

> *The Lord now chose seventy-two other disciples*
> *and sent them ahead in pairs to all the towns*
> *and places he planned to visit.*
> Luke 10:1

> *When the seventy-two disciples returned,*
> *they joyfully reported him, "Lord,*
> *even* ***the demons obey us*** *when we use your name!"*
> Luke 10:17

Wow! What powerful statements.

Remember, I want to encourage you to take the Word of God serious and I want to challenge you to become a "real ghost buster" for Jesus.

Reports of liberation

Report:

Nightmares
One day a young woman came to us and asked us for help because she had terrible nightmares. She saw ugly faces in her dreams and felt depression and fear of life generally. First we prayed for discernment about where these things came from. Because demons need an entrance to come into people's lives. Then the woman told us that her boyfriend dearly liked watching horror movies and he more or less made her watching them with him. She did it for his sake but actually she felt disgust for these movies.
So we lead her to repentance for this very thing and later commanded these powers to leave her life in the Name of Jesus.

Immediately she felt something evil leaving her. From that very moment she never had nightmares again, and did not watch horror movies anymore.
Jesus sets free!

3-year old boy wins
Oh, and there is one more fantastic incident I remember.
We visited believing friends, had just had dinner and their son who was about 3 years old, was taken to bed. After some time, he came downstairs again, crying and completely distraught. When his mom asked him what had happened, he sobbingly said: "There is such an evil thing in my room and it frightens me." We talked to him and could calm him down. Because he already knew about Jesus we explained the power of the Name of Jesus to him and that he should send away this evil thing if it came back again.
We said it first and he repeated: "You evil thing – leave, in

the Name of Jesus!" Really simple, suitable for a child and effective.

Beaming with joy, he rushed away upstairs to his room again. For a while we did not hear anything from him anymore and we thought the incident was over. Suddenly he came down into the living room once again and he indignantly said: "The evil thing is still there but I forgot what to say."
Once more we explained it to him. Very motivated he went up to his room again. During the whole evening we did not hear anything from him anymore.

The next day we met his mom and wanted to know if her boy had come to her again last night. She told us that he had been in his room the whole night long. When he had come downstairs in the morning she asked him about the "evil thing". Happily he had told her, "the evil thing" had still been there when he came up the second time, but he loudly said the sentence we had told him. "You evil thing – leave, in the Name of Jesus!". Immediately it had left and never returned again.

A little boy used the name of Jesus trusting in it and he had peace.

We've experienced things like that very often. Childlike trust and acting on the bible produced biblical results. Jesus did not undervalue children.
Unless you become like children...

> *Then he (Jesus) said, "I tell you the truth,*
> *unless you turn from your sins and become*
> *like little children,*
> *you will never get into the Kingdom of Heaven."*
> Matthew 18:3

It is not meant to become "childish" but to have childlike trust.
No idea about anything but boldly go because Daddy is there and he is in control. And my Daddy is the strongest anyway, and he can do everything.

Turn from what? From the things that stand in our way and block us with regards to the Kingdom of God and its principles.
We need a logical and scientific explanation for everything, a reason for everything and much more.

How different children are in this aspect? "Daddy said it, so it is right and I believe it!"

Right? Have you experienced something like that with children? Certainly. What a statement – and that is exactly why Jesus takes children as an example.

And that was exactly why I have taken God at his Word too, because HE had said it this way and also meant it like that. That is why I started this exciting journey into the adventure-land of faith.
Come and join me!

Stronger than expected
We were in a service of a church we befriended in La Plata / Argentina. After the preaching we had a time of serving the people with prayer and I noticed a young man who was leaning at the wall, totally uninterested, while all around him healing wonders were taking place, people falling down, cheering, crying for joy and much more.
One woman came up to me, asking me to pray for this young man, it was her son.

So I went to him and asked if it was alright if I prayed for him. Bored he shrugged his shoulders looking at me with these strange dark eyes. At that very moment his eye color was almost deeply black.

I took a closer look at that guy. He was quite scruffy, smelling of alcohol and marijuana. His whole appearance made me know he surely did not know Jesus yet and he was really addicted and intoxicated at that moment.

I prayed, asking: Lord, what shall I do – this boy needs help! Jesus said: "Just lay your hand onto his shoulder and then entrust him to me."

As I interpreted his shoulder-shrugging as an agreement with my prayer, I laid my hand onto his shoulder and said "Jesus, please show him your love and your power!"

Then I stepped back, waiting. He was stood there and was not moving anymore. He seemed to be like thunderstruck. Suddenly he started shaking, sweating from every pore and could hardly stand. Then he started screaming in a way I had never heard before. It was an inhuman, fiendish scream.

At that moment I knew that demons were manifesting because they were confronted with Jesus.
He became wild, madly waving his arms he lashed around, had foam on his mouth and wildly thrashing around he fell to the ground. The whole time he was screaming.

He was grabbed by some "stewards" of the church and pulled out of the crowd. Four or five of them could hardly hold him. They brought him into a side-room where they set him free from the demons within a short time.

He gave his life to Jesus, received HIM as his savior and liberator and he was normal. I was amazed at Jesus, how HE had done that. No power is stronger than Jesus.

This experience made me think of reports from the New Testament where you can read:

Jesus and his companions went to the town of Capernaum.
When the Sabbath day came,
he went into the synagogue and began to teach.
The people were amazed at his teaching,
for he taught with real authority -
quite unlike the teachers of religious law.
Suddenly, a man in the synagogue who was possessed
by an unclean spirit began shouting,
"Why are you interfering with us, Jesus of Nazareth?
Have you come to destroy us?
I know who you are – the Holy One sent from God!".
Jesus cut him short.
"Be quiet! Come out of the man," he ordered.
At that, the evil spirit screamed,
threw the man into a convulsion,
and then came out of him.
Mark 1:21-26

Jesus has got all the power and the demons tremble at His Name.

I do not know whether you might be addicted or stuck in bondage but Jesus wants to set you free. Therefore, he hung on the cross and he let himself be killed for you to have life. No matter what it is: alcohol, drugs, fears, phobias, there is nothing Jesus did not handle and finish. Nothing is too persistent or too strong to be able to withstand the power of Jesus.

Shopaholic

Some time ago a young woman came to my wife and I, admitting that she was a shopaholic. She could not resist, if she saw something nice in a magazine she had to buy or order it. It was the same when she was in a store. She knew that this was not normal, all of her money went out and she was not free. She terribly suffered under this condition.
Andra ordered freedom from this bondage in Jesus' Name. Immediately the woman felt a change. She went home and for the first time in many years she could throw away magazines and was set free from that moment.

Jesus is the absolute chain breaker!

For you have been called to live in freedom, my brothers and sisters. ...
Galatians 5:13a

So Christ has truly set us free! Now make sure that you stay free, and don't get tied up again in slavery to the law.
Galatians 5:1

Here we have it in black and white. We should be free and Jesus has set us free. The preconditions are given, come and get this freedom from Jesus. People experience it every day – so why not you as well!

Ignorance and silence

Diseases instead of hope

I find it is very interesting to listen to people. On the bus, in the swimming pool, on a shopping tour and so on. Most of the time they are talking about diseases and exchanging the latest news. It seems to be absolutely normal; they have got used to it, they have got topics to talk about and they try everything to find help, even if it is the craziest therapies.
However, when you start a conversation telling them that Jesus can heal them and ask to pray for them, very often it is seen as – "erroneous and too extreme".

But what is the reason for that?

People believe what they have heard a lot of. They are influenced by advertisement and personal experiences learned from each other. You talk about the things that apparently already helped and what individuals are convinced of. That is the norm.

For the most part, the power of the Gospel got lost in the last 1700 years. The first church lived with an absolute certainty of the power of Jesus and used it to serve the people. So many healing wonders and miracles happened that whole areas heard about it and saw amazing wonders. It caused greatest joy among the population.

We have to think intensively about and imagine the following reports! A man comes along, proclaiming Jesus and the Kingdom of God with such a power that everyone is open-mouthed – and after that, all are enthusiastic, giving their lives to Jesus. What a change in people and society.
Read it for yourself and be astonished:

*Philip, for example, went to the city of Samaria
and told the people there about the Messiah.
Crowds listened intently to Philip
because they were eager to **hear** his message and
see the miraculous signs **he did**.
Many unclean spirits were cast out,
screaming as they left their victims.
And many who had been paralyzed or
lame were healed.
So there was **great joy in that city**.*

*A man named Simon had been a sorcerer there
for many years, amazing the people of Samaria
and claiming to be someone great.
Everyone, from the least to the greatest,
often spoke of him as
"the Great One – the Power of God".
They listened closely to him because
for a long time he had astounded them with his magic.
But now the people believed Philip's **message**
of Good News concerning the
Kingdom of God and the **name of Jesus Christ**.
As a result, many men and women were baptized.
Then Simon himself believed and was baptized.
He began following Philip
wherever he went, and he was amazed
by the signs and great miracles Philip **performed**.*
Acts 8:5-13

*But (despite Jesus' instructions),
the **report of his power** spread even faster,
and vast crowds came **to hear** him preach and
to **be healed** of their diseases.*
Luke 5:15

What for heaven's sake could it be that we do not know this anymore today? The explanations are various and it would fill a whole book describing them. Anyway, it is a fact, that this dimension of faith in all its power is not known anymore by most part of the population. We do not publicly speak about our faith anymore after a Chancellor once said, this was "privacy and not for publicity".

Thank God, there are churches, parishes and individuals who did not stop believing in the Word of God and using the power of the Holy Spirit, the power and authority of the Name of Jesus and talking about it. More and more wonders are happening, as in biblical times.

We should start to talk again about a Jesus who has not changed and we should make that known everywhere we go.

Jesus Christ is the same
yesterday, today and forever.
Hebrews 13:8

But how can they call on him to save them
unless they believe in him?
And how can they believe in him if they have never heard
about him?
And how can they hear about him
unless someone tells them?
Romans 10:14

The people captured by their needs, problems, addictions, diseases and fears shall hear that still today, there is a way. This way is called:

Jesus Christ, the Son of God!

Dramatically misguided

This way has not changed the last 2000 years. History teaches us that a lot of wrong things have been done by the spiritual leaders of the decades and there has been a lot of sin and fault. Jesus has not been ministered, although it was said to be done "in His Name".

Still today, however, so called "spiritual leaders" mess up the real goal, claiming Jesus not to be the son of God. Eventually, this is the logical conclusion to the statement: "Jesus was not conceived by the Holy Spirit but by Joseph." As a result, he was not the son of God, as a result, he was not the savior, as a result, all the reports written in the Bible were not true and you were not entitled to take it.

Poor Germany! Poor people believing that; poor "spiritual leaders" who are ultimately responsible before God for having told so many people untruths and having lead them into temptation.
They are blocking so many people. Hope for help is being destroyed, the people have to endure their pain. In the end they go to hell because they have been kept away from Jesus or they have been told bad things about him. That is the actual big drama.

As long as the people hear preaching from behind the pulpits, honoring every labor union or every Environmental Protection Association but they do not hear anything about the gift of grace and salvation through Jesus, we are far away from the power and change through Jesus. Of course, these topics might also be important but how does it help a person if he/she does not know Jesus.

What use is a rescued animal species have if you are lost and have to spend eternity in hell, separated from God.

Some time ago I got a church letter (I better not mention the name of this parish), which was great – well presented.
High shine – pictures – reports – fifteen pages long – but not once Jesus was mentioned, let alone that HE wants to care about the needs of the church members. The impression Christians can give is more than sad, although they should know **Christ**.

Still, over the decades there have always been people experiencing him and also spreading that. Thank God. Still today. Thank you, Lord!

These days we can see an increasing number of godly healing wonders and reports all over the world because humans rediscover this power and truth of the Gospel, talking about it.

Why does the media report about it so little? I do not know. There could be many reasons for it but they are just speculative.

But thank God we do not depend on the media, very often it is only partly telling the truth, above all from a subjective perspective. Even if they do not report about followers of Jesus in a very kind way.

So that is why I am writing about all the various reports of healing and Jesus stepping in! Reports about people who are getting new hope and trusting Jesus - that HE can and wants to help them. People spreading what their life was like before and how Jesus has changed it into something good.

Here you could write down some examples of media reports that talk about miracles through Jesus. I hope that this page does not stay white.

Healing reports Part III

Crooked hip straight again -
life is easier again

Report of a 43-year old woman:

I would like to tell you about two healing wonders that I experienced in the church.

Only a few months ago I came to a living faith in Jesus and since then I have been going to church as well.

In the past I was always wondering why my trousers were cut crooked when I was bought new ones. One pant leg was always longer than the other one. Each time I had to order a dress maker to equalize both pant legs. But with the time I got hip pain, so it dawned on me that possibly one leg was too short. I got it checked – I had a tilted pelvis.

In one of the healing services, one of the elders prayed for my hip and immediately I felt that something was happening with it. It rumbled and after a short time the pains were gone and both of my legs had the same length. When I bought my next pair of trousers I noticed that both pant legs were aligned. What a surprise.

The second thing was that after an accident I had a stiffening in the spine. Sleeping, I could not lay on my back and I also could not bend forward.

In this case as well, I trusted in prayer in church and again I was prayed for by the same female elder. Right after prayer she asked me to do what I had not been able to before – bend forward.

First I thought: My God – you just cannot. But because of the encouraging prayer my faith was so big that I dared to. Carefully I bend down – it worked – Hallelujah! More and more energetically I repeated and yet more and more vigorously.

After a few days I recognized that I could sleep on my back again too – without any problems.

I am so thankful to God that he heals, that he has saved me, that I have got a church where you can personally experience Jesus and that there are people talking about this Jesus in an understandable and totally relaxed way. Laying their hands upon the sick and praying with great enthusiasm, expectation and success.

Two other people experienced a similar thing when Andra and I were in Wels / Austria. It was only a short time ago.

Bending forward like never before -
childhood dreams come true

Report:

Before I prayed for her, a young woman gave us a short report about her problem.
Since her earliest childhood the doctors had realized that one of her legs was too short. She had to wear balancing soles or shoes but later she left them out because it did not look nice and, after all, she was a pretty lady.

The results were a crooked hip position, lumbar osteoarthritis, a lot of physiotherapy and – last but not least – a stiffening of the lumbar region. On top of this she had a lot of pain, suffering, limitation and much more. The consequence:

> She could not bend down anymore!

During prayer she started bending forward – on and on and on – until she could touch the floor with her fingertips. she had not been able to do that since her childhood.

She demonstrated it many times in front of the whole church. Her back was elastic again and completely free of pain.
This was on a Saturday.

Jesus is a fantastic therapist!!!!!

"I also want to be able to do that"

On Sunday morning after the preaching, an older man came to the front and crying he asked for prayer. He also wanted to be able to bend down like this.

During the preaching I had called the young woman to the front to confirm the miracle again. She came and once again showed the whole church how effortlessly she could bend down to the floor now. Moreover, she explained that her whole family had checked whether one leg was still too short. Every one of them were familiar with her condition. It was not.

Because of this demonstration the man was so moved that hope and faith had filled his heart. Since he was a child he had had a stiffed back and he **had never been able** to bend down.
What drama and agony his whole life! He was about 60 – 70 years old.

I prayed for him and during prayer he started bending forward until he could clasp his ankles. He was crying even more – now because of joy!

There was such a great joy in the church, everyone was praising Jesus.
I was absolutely enthusiastic how Jesus had healed two people just like that and how he had made them incredibly happy.

All honor be to Jesus!!!!

Sciatic pain ...

A 56-year old woman reporting from the healing service, 31st May 2015

The last few weeks I noticed increasing aches in my back. It got worse and worse until the diagnosis of the doctor was:

it was Sciatica!
Great!

I could hardly bend down, every single movement hurt.

I was finally prayed for in a healing service at the church. The wife of the pastor laid her hands upon me and prayed in the Name of Jesus.

Immediately every pain was gone. I could feel it at once. I bend down to test it.
I had completely painless mobility.

Later at home, I tried it out and the pain was and has stayed gone.

I give all honor to Jesus.

Chocolate allergy …
An 8-year old girl reports from a service, 25th May 2015

In one of our services, an 8-year old girl came to the front with her father for prayer.
They had realized that for some time now that she was allergic to chocolate and some other cocoa products.
After each consumption of chocolate products, she immediately broke out into a severe rush.

This wasn't nice for the girl nor a good outlook for the future. Her father saw it the same way. An allergy would only unnecessarily put a strain on their family life.

So the wife of the pastor prayed for her and ordered the allergy to leave in Jesus' name.

Home again, the small one immediately ate sweet things with chocolate – without any allergic physical reactions.
With joy and delight she tried it once again one week later.
The allergic reaction stayed gone.

You can probably imagine the joy and thankfulness of the little girl. And of her parents!

Thank God!

Once again, we asked the girl and her parents about it some weeks later. Everything is in perfect order, the allergy has left.

… and backaches leave!

A 40-year old woman reports from a service at Mallorca, May 2015

We visited the church "Esperanza de Vida" in Cala Ratjada. So after the preaching during a service, we prayed for various people with various of prayer requests.

A 40-year old woman came to us explaining her problem. She had chronic, painful backache which occurred again and again seemingly without any reason.
At that moment she had severe backache.

Right after prayer it did not seem to change a lot, the pains were still there, but at least a bit less than before.

When we met her the following week, she told us she had not thought about it. Suddenly she was aware of that and when she thought about it she realized that the backache was gone and that she had been free of pain the whole week.
It hadn't been like that for months now.

She was extremely happy and gave all thanks and honor to Jesus.

Sun allergy leaving -
why vacation is fun again

Report:

Some time ago an acquaintance of mine told me that she was going on vacation to Egypt. She was absolutely looking forward to seeing this country - the Red Sea, scuba diving, the fish and swimming.

She only had one problem: for many years now she had a sun allergy and needed a special cream for protection. But even that did not help 100 percent. In the sun, these ugly, itching pustules came up.

I offered to pray for her because I was convinced that this allergy was no problem for Jesus.

She gave me her hand and I commanded this allergy to leave in the Name of Jesus. All done in a totally non-religious and unspectacular way and following that I wished her a nice vacation.

When we met about three weeks later, she enthusiastically told me that the prayer had worked. Every day she had been in the sun.
No allergic reaction. She had literally searched for the pustules but not found them. She had been convinced that there still had to be some because there had always been some in the sun.
But there was nothing visible nor perceptible.

Jesus had offered her a carefree vacation and given me a good possibility to go on talking with her about Jesus. Only with one more convincing argument now.

The Great Commission

Go …

Again and again we are surprised about all the things that happen. Although not everything has been healed yet, nevertheless quite a lot of things have been.
This encourages us to keep on praying, trusting Jesus for more and greater things and giving hope to the people.

There is no formula or you-have-to-do-it-like-this.
It is the things Jesus had told his disciples, put into practice. Please recognize that Jesus did neither "recommend" it to them nor give any option. It was a commandment.

We cannot call Jesus our "Lord" if we then do not do what he told us. HE is the "boss", we are the assistants. HE is in the driver's seat, so do we do it or well, let's see – maybe not? This doesn't go together somehow. And that is exactly the "difficulty": to perceive, where do I not obey the will of Jesus, maybe where I do it partly or where I do it without any enthusiasm and faith.

My own experience clearly shows that. I did not have this understanding for miracles, let alone did I pray with faith for healing and liberation in the described way. But thank God, this has changed.
Jesus is patient, merciful and forgiving. Still HE encourages and helps me to go on and to conquer unknown dimensions.

Each time we have prayed for people, they at least got attention and the feeling that someone cared about them and their problems. In most cases they later told us that they felt the power of God, very often combined with physical welfare and warmth or heat in the affected area. Even if they did not receive healing at once, they were encouraged to cling to it because very often the process of healing had just started. At the very least they felt God's touch.

Here I would like to remind you of my previously mentioned report about the young ex-wheelchair user in La Plata, Argentina.

The commission Jesus gave to his disciples – to this very day – still says the following:

> *And then he (Jesus) told them:*
> *Go into all the world and preach the Gospel to everyone.*
> *Anyone who believes and is baptized will be saved.*
> *But anyone who refuses to believe will be condemned.*
> *These miraculous signs will accompany*
> *those who believe:*
> *they will cast out demons in my name,*
> *and they will speak in new tongues.*
> *They will be able to handle snakes with safety,*
> *and if they drink anything poisonous, it won't hurt them.*
> *They will be able to place their hands*
> *on the sick, and they will be healed."*
> *when the Lord Jesus had finished talking with them,*
> *he was taken up into heaven and sat down*
> *in the place of honor at God's right hand.*
> *And the disciples went everywhere*
> *and preached, and the Lord*
> *worked through them, confirming what they said*
> *by many miraculous signs.*
> Mark 16:15-20

It is quite simple and not theologically complicated:
Jesus gave an order – his disciples were supposed to carry out – and Jesus cares about the results.
My responsibility is just putting this into practice, trusting in and obeying to his Word. And that is the process of learning, the fight, the questions and doubts – but still not to give up.

This is your and my challenge!

Among other things, the Great Commission includes two important facts.
"Go and preach" and "demonstrate the power of Jesus". Both belong together. That is how Jesus acted, the same way his disciples did, and that is how we should act too!

It was really important to Paul to explicitly emphasize that he did not only talk piously.

> *And my message and my preaching were very plain.*
> *Rather than using clever and persuasive speeches,*
> *I relied only on the power of the Holy Spirit.*
> 1. Corinthians 2:4

A lot of other examples given in the Bible show us this connection of saying and doing.

> *Crowds listened intently to Philip because*
> *they were eager to hear his message and see the miraculous signs he did.*
> Acts 8:6

As proof of what they had said before, they demonstrated the power (Greek: dynamis). It was literally like dynamite, blasting many doubts and blockages, idols and wrong religious ideas, and setting people free so they believed in Jesus. This combination is unique in the world of religions and it is still potent.

What, if nothing happens?

I have been asked many times whether I am a miracle worker. Frequently I answered no, giving the hint that I knew the "miracle worker" very well and that I have been traveling around for him.
Jesus alone has got the power and strength. I just try to do what he has ordered and authorized me to.

When I first started praying for the sick, a quiet thought arose in my head, asking:

"What, if nothing happens? Then you will have made a fool of yourself!"

At first I let myself be hindered by these thoughts because they sounded plausible. Indeed, I would look like an idiot, I would not have the words to explain. My thoughts were racing and they got louder and louder because of all the "ifs" and "buts". How would the people react? Would they ever come to Jesus again? So many open questions finally kept me off praying for people.

If you are already a follower of Jesus and you decide to put the Great Commission into practice, I can promise you one thing: This question will bombard you:

What, if nothing happens?

Still today, after all the experiences and fantastic miracles and wonders, very often this thought wants to come just before I pray.
But today, I just laugh about it, thinking: "Yeah, old devil, you'd like that, wouldn't you? No chance! I will pray and God is there to do good things to the people." And then, determined, I lay my hands upon them and command in the Name of Jesus.

In fact:
- for Jesus to be honored
- according to his word
- for the sake of the one I'm praying for
- to provoke the one who wants to discourage me
- to prove: Jesus is the winner and the devil is the eternal looser
- as an encouragement for those who watch
- as a role model for insecure Christians to copy

Something is happening!

You have to find it out yourself. I can only tell you my story, showing how it was at first, what I experienced and how I got into this new dimension.

You must get in the Word of God yourself, learning what it means to have authority and to also use it, discovering spiritual truths and principles for you, so you can eventually find a way to put them into practice. Finding answers and convictions, which do not throw you off balance or leave you out in the rain with depressive, helpless thoughts any longer, so you can hold your head high and boldly say:

> "If nothing happens?
> Really easy – nothing happens.
> But something will happen 100 percent,
> because it is the responsibility of Jesus.
> When I pray for somebody – and I definitely will –
> at least he/she will experience
> the love of God and even more!"

It is time for us as Christians from all backgrounds, to learn that again. To not be held back by the question "... if nothing happens", and not to allow this little question to frighten or paralyze us, so the people cannot perceive the Jesus of the Bible.

I pray for You to break through this merry-go-round of your thoughts and to get such a certainty that Jesus is always for you and by your side.

I want this book to encourage and motivate you, to go on and to discover the dimensions of the Kingdom of God, learning and putting them into practice and to become strong in the Holy Spirit.

Or you just realize that nothing is impossible for Jesus and that you can give your life to him without worries.

Just write down which thoughts turn over in your mind when you think about praying for someone.

What prevents you?

How have you been influenced? What shakes your image of God or your understanding of faith, based on that?

Can you imagine doing the signs and wonders of Jesus too?

So in connection to that, I also understand the following reports, happened in some services we had in Brazil, Spain and Austria.

Healing reports Part IV

Report:

Finger tendon growing together

In a service in Brazil I was preaching about the power of Jesus and that he still healed people today. I saw a man with a thick bandage around his right hand.

So I interrupted the preaching because suddenly I knew that Jesus wanted to do something now. As I asked the man what had happened and he explained that all his finger tendons were cut and that he could not move the fingers anymore.

The doctors doubted it would ever be cured. Many operations were necessary and everything was costly and unsure. In the best case there would be at least a strong impairment.

At that moment his fingers were just hanging limply out of the bandage.

I prayed with him and commanded the tendons to grow together again, in Jesus' Name.
Then I went on with the preaching.

After a few minutes he lifted up his bandaged hand without saying a word. First I thought he wanted to ask me something, then I realized he was moving his fingers, for everyone in the church to see. The church started cheering because they knew the man and his problem.

Later he told me that right after prayer he noticed how something had changed in his injured hand.

Bent shoulder straight again

Maybe it was the most impressive healing that happened in the first few months of the year 2013 in a church in Brazil. A nearly 70-year old man had broken his shoulder a few months ago, however, he had no money to go to the doctor, let alone to have an injury insurance.
The complicated fracture in the shoulder had grown together in such a twisted way that the man could not use his arm anymore because the shoulder was stiff and completely out of order. The man could neither lift his arm, nor rotate, nor bend the elbow, even his wrist was stiff.
The only possibility would have been that somebody would pay for hospitalization and the doctors break the wrong bones check and align them, hoping for it to be cured again.

But Jesus had an amazing alternative for this man!
I prayed for him, laid my hand upon his deformed shoulder and commanded the bones to come into normal order again and to get straight in the Name of Jesus.
I was commanding with the authority Jesus has given to me, speaking mobility into the whole shoulder area, into the tendons, wrists, ankles and the bones.
When I laid my hands on his shoulder, I could feel something jerk and the bones move.
Jesus just was doing something.

Sometime later, everyone in the room was overwhelmed to see the man lifting his arm, twisting and finally spinning it around like a windmill. He just did not want to stop. At the same time, tears of joy were running down his aged, furrowed face.
He gave praise to God from the bottom of his heart.
And the whole church was cheering with excitement and thanking God.

Old lady jumping like a girl

One Sunday an old woman came to a service in Porto Cristo, Mallorca, walking on two crutches.
She could hardly move her knees and dragged herself along. For years now she had been suffering with severe arthritis and had tremendous pain in her knees. So that was how she dragged herself along to service each Sunday.

We commanded the spirit of arthritis to leave the woman and immediately she felt new strength flowing into her knees. The pain left and she started walking, bending her knees and lifting them up.

She handed her crutches over to Andra and walked faster and faster without them, it looked like a folk dance. She was beaming and thanking Jesus.

I took her arm and we were walking through the whole church, getting faster and faster. Eventually we were running through the service room, with the church breaking into cheers.

At the end of the service she went home with the crutches under her arm. There was no hint of walking difficulties or pains.

A morning in the mountains…

After one service in Wels, Austria, a middle-aged man came to the front for prayer. He told us that he absolutely loved to go hiking in the mountains.
(Of course: Austria – mountains – nature – everything fine!)

However, he had damaged knees and he could hardly move them. The doctors had given him quite a gloomy prediction for his future.

One knee had a damaged kneecap and meniscus, the other one had been realized to have a fluid in the bone marrow.
I had no idea what that was, but at that very moment I did not care, anyway. Later I did some research on the internet about the diagnosis, it was:
medical definition: increased water retention inside of the bone, indicating through increased signal intensity in the water sensitive sequences of the Magnetic Resonance Imaging, based on an edema or hematoma formation in the bone.
It definitely did not sound good!

So he asked for prayer because he would love to go out into nature again and to get rid of the pains and problems.
Andra and I prayed for him and laid our hands upon him in the Name of Jesus. Evidently, nothing had happened. He had not noticed any change and had not felt anything during prayer, but he was still absolutely encouraged because he knew Jesus would take care of him. Then he went home.

The same day he let us know by phone that he was completely healed, could walk and move his knees without any pain. When he had come home from service, everything had been alright.

Jesus gave him the chance to enjoy His beautiful creation by going hiking in the mountains again

Two years later, when we were in the same church in Wels, he rushed up to us, beaming, and gratefully shook our hands. He was so happy, he was doing incredibly fine, his knees were working normally and painlessly and he was able to move them just fine. He had already done a lot, including part of a difficult hiking tour.

The great thing was, that this healing made his son come back to Jesus again. He had been educated as a Christian, but then went on his way without God. Because of his father's healing, he had been confronted with Jesus in such a strong way that he returned, repented and is now going to church and trusting Jesus more than ever before.

So this once more shows that God has his own way of helping people. No going by the book. No thinking that God is a machine – throw a prayer into it and healing automatically comes out. No! It is about trust.

Here you can see the tension I already mentioned and which you experience if you are praying for others. If you do not see something at once or do not feel anything, nevertheless, something is happening. Imagine if we had not prayed for that man. That wouldn't have turned out well.

Young wheelchair user walking again

This is a report about what happened in Mallorca in November 2013.

A 16-year old girl had been seriously injured by a balcony fall from the second floor.
For hours she had been operated on and among other things her left foot had been completely destroyed. The doctors had told her the fractures were so disastrous that they were inoperable, which meant that she would never be able to step on this foot again. As a result, she would never be able to walk again. The bones in her feet were literally pulverized, so there was nothing left to be put together.
Her mother later described it as a really smashed up pumice stone. A lot of little crumbs.

As a result of that, the family had to change their whole life circumstances, and think about how they could adapt. They would have to move to a wheelchair-friendly apartment at ground level, buy an appropriate car, a wheelchair-friendly reorganization of the new flat, financing everything and much more. Suddenly a huge mountain appeared in front of the family.

At this point in time, Andra and I were on our very first conference called "Mas Fuego – Mas Gloria", in English: "More fire – more glory", in Cala Ratjada, Mallorca.
We had invited our dear friends, pastors from La Plata, Argentina, to serve the people, who gathered together from different churches.
Pastor Raul and Betty Reyes have been our friends for many years now and they are the leaders of a thriving church, with about 2500 members at the moment.
In their services they also witness a lot of healing, signs and wonders.

Saturday evening the girl came in her wheelchair with her family. The local pastor, in whose church we had the conference, had invited the family. Suddenly I knew that she would be healed tonight and I was looking forward to this service.
I was ready!

On this evening, Pastor Raul was preaching about the demonstration of the power of God and he suddenly went to the teenager in the wheelchair. I recognized what he planned to do now.
Darn it – he had been faster than me!

But thank God it was not about me, but about the girl and Jesus.

So he prayed for her, took her hand and told her to get up in the Name of Jesus.

You could have heard a pin drop in the church. Eyes were wide open up, hands held in front of mouths not to scream, the tension was immense and it was utterly still.

The girl was shaken by the power of God and then slowly started to arise, mainly using her healthy foot. Obviously, she did not trust the whole thing yet. But then she started to put weight on the left, damaged foot and her amazement grew.
She stood on her foot with all her weight. So with Pastor Raul holding her hand she started to walk.
She cried because of joy and thankfulness, totally overwhelmed.
They carefully walked through the room.

By now her parents, brothers and sisters and many other visitors were crying.

Later Pastor Lorenzo told us that she was now walking at home as well. On Sunday and on the following days.

A visit at the doctors brought great confusion – for the doc!
He X-rayed the foot, let the analyzed picture be thrown away, X-rayed again and again and he could not get it. In his opinion the X-ray machine was out of order. The foot had been completely healed, all bones had grown together and were in order. He even suspected the girl to be another patient. The doctor ordered more checkups.

The news of the healing of the girl spread in the whole city because her accident and its consequences had already been in the press. A lot of people, who didn't even really believe in God, were talking of a healing miracle. For the whole church there were a lot of good chances to talk about Jesus with them.

In January 2014, the family not only testified what an amazing miracle Jesus had done to the daughter, to the church but they also gave an interview to the local magazine, "Faxdepera". It was about two and a half DIN A4 pages long, with photos and the medical findings.
(As a reminder and confirmation we kept one copy.)

Jesus is so wonderful!

I love him and I absolutely love to be there when he does miracles.

So think for a second – which positive side effects this healing had for the whole family and all the people involved. No move to a disability-friendly apartment necessary, no special car, no rehabilitation for her whole lifetime, just the positive financial aspect alone is huge.

Imagine, what the health insurance has saved. Count it up to about 70 years' life expectancy. It would be more than €100.000, no doubt. Actually, the doctor and his assistants should give their lives to Jesus.

> *A vast crowd brought to him (Jesus)*
> *people who were lame, blind, crippled,*
> *those who couldn't speak, and many others.*
> *They laid them before Jesus, and he healed them all.*
> *The crowd was amazed!*
> *Those who hadn't been able to speak were talking,*
> *the crippled were made well,*
> *the lame were walking, and the blind could see again!*
> *And they praised the God of Israel.*
> Matthew 15:30+31

This was written about 2000 years ago because the disciples experienced it with Jesus exactly that way. They were by his side, so they also were eye witnesses of the things that were happening.

And today it is us who testify of the same things because we have personally seen it with our own eyes.

- That doesn't happen! -We are eye witnesses!
- I can't believe it! - We are eye witnesses!
- You cannot take these things literally today! - We are eye witnesses!
- We – experienced – it!!!

Oh yes, by the way, the scripture above is talking about dumb people speaking again at once.

A dumb person speaking

In 2010, we were at one of the biggest conferences in Argentina, preaching, teaching and praying for the people.

One evening a young girl came to the front with her mother for prayer, she was maybe about 10 years old. There was a quite big crowd, a lot of people needed and wanted prayer. It was very loud.

The mother and her daughter stood in front of Andra. The mother explained everything in Spanish, pointed at her girl, kept on speaking and gesticulating. But because of the lack of a translator at that very moment and the noise around her, Andra did not know what the problem was that the mother was trying to explain. The daughter did not say anything. But it did not matter – Jesus had understood what it was.

Andra prayed for the girl and suddenly she started talking to Andra in Spanish. The mother was beside herself, so we asked what it was.
The mom told us her daughter had been dumb and had never spoken yet in her whole life. Now she could and had also demonstrated it to Andra publicly.

All honor be to Jesus. He is proving that his word has not lost any of its power and message (look above).

Legs straight again

At the same conference I also prayed for a teenaged girl whose feet or legs were twisted so much that she could not walk normally, but tripped over her own feet and fell very often.
Naturally, that hindered her and she was teased by other teenagers laughing at her. Above all, this just did not look nice for a young lady.

I prayed for the legs in the Name of Jesus, to straighten.
The left leg immediately straightened with only one quick movement. The right leg stayed twisted. It still looked strange, but not that terrible anymore - half of it was already done. The girl was so happy and she could walk in a much better way.

I encouraged her to come the next evening if there was no change overnight, that we would pray for her once more and Jesus would definitely finish it.

The next evening, she stood in front of me again, her left leg was still as straight. It had not deteriorated. So I prayed for the right leg and within a second it was as straight as the other one.
Jesus had healed her in "two steps".

Maybe you're wondering - why?
I don't know.
But what I know is that Jesus has no method or ways of doing it by numbers, but HE serves each person personally and individually, as they put their trust in him. That is why it is so exciting to pray for people. You must listen to Jesus and to what HE wants to do right now and in which way.

Straight-eyed

At the conference there was also a little boy maybe 5 or 6 years old who came to us and he looked straight into my eyes.

Mamma mia! He did not need to tell me what his prayer request was, it was obvious! With his left eye he was virtually looking into his right trousers pockets. The left eye was cross-eyed like I had never seen it before.

I laid my hand upon the affected eye and prayed for him. Immediately after I had taken away my hand and had commanded the eye to look straight in Jesus' name, the eye looked straight ahead. His gaze was normal.

It was fantastic to see.

Amazing development

Step by step

Looking back to all these years, I can see how Jesus lead me step by step. HE revealed truths and principles of his Word to me and helped me to put them into practice.
I would have never dreamed that one day I would experience things like the aforementioned ones in this book. And yet it is true. It makes me increasingly enthusiastic. In our church, wherever we serve, wherever we talk to people, we pray with them.

Not only quantity but also the quality has intensified.
At the beginning only "little things" left, such as headaches, pain in the body and things like that but later the healing miracles also got "bigger", the longer we went on praying for people in the Name of Jesus. We never gave up, even if we did not see any results.

You have read yourself, what we described up to now and what we have already experienced.

It is also very interesting for me to see; I am not the only one. I am getting to know more and more people who have experienced a similar development in their lives, still standing in this process of learning. Healing wonders, miracles and God stepping in, is increasing more and more in the churches, letting the Holy Spirit have his way.

And it occurs at any time. There were strong healing-movements in the 1940s, 50s and at other times, so thousands of people got to know Jesus and received him as their Lord.

Back to the power

It is the wish of God for his church. For his children and representatives here on earth. We have got a strong, supernatural God who does signs and wonders! The Holy Spirit is about to restore the power of the first church doing miracles. As a follower of Jesus you are called to represent God in a way that is worthy of him; the Bible speaks really clearly about that. Of course, there are special callings and anointings, but there is also a basic order and basic equipment for every single Christian.

For example, some are evangelists with a special mission but all Christians are challenged to preach the Gospel. It is the same with a lot of other callings.

Acts 29

If you look up Acts 29 in your bible, you might be surprised to see that there actually is no such chapter.

What? What about that? Are you kidding me?

The explanation therefore is quite easy. The Book of Acts describes the birth of the first church, how it behaved, its development and the behaviour of individuals and whole groups in authority and power.

It describes the triumphant invasion of the Gospel of Jesus and the Kingdom of God and it is full of descriptions of signs and wonders, which captivated all of society.
Ok – there were people who did not want that and who fought against the church. That is nothing new.

I (Jesus) tell you the truth,
anyone who believes in me will do
the same works I have done, and even greater works,
because I am going to be with the Father.
John 14:12

Wow! I am miles away from that. But this is the will of Jesus explained, for my life and also for yours. "Anyone who believes in me" is the only condition for that. The difference between Jesus' statement and my behaviour is the place to learn.

Chapter 29 is **YOUR** chapter, where God wants you to write it. To fill this chapter with your experiences, so other people will get motivated to come to Jesus and to experience his power. Your life should be filled with supernatural experiences because you have got a supernatural God as your Lord and you are serving him. Of course, my life should be like that too.

Do not tell God what to do

In early years I was so often told that I mustn't and couldn't tell God what to do. This is absolutely true and right. However, the context of this statement was that it was said after I had prayed trusting in his Word.

For example, I prayed for a sick person, saying: It is written that through his stripes we are healed. Be healed in Jesus' Name.

That was at the very beginning of what I just described. Very often, a statement came up like "You cannot tell or force God that HE should do anything."

First, I was impressed by that because I also heard it from

spiritual leaders and I thought, "they are probably right". But then, Jesus showed me that this statement was like a brake in my life. I would not expect anything anymore, would give all the authority away, actually given to me by Jesus, so eventually I would blame God for it because HE did not do anything, I mean I could not help it. I would be off the hook.

Let me illustrate that to you with an example.
You are offered a great new car, with all bells and whistles. Just everything – Wow!
Then you read the user guide (you've got to do that) and you perceive: Man – it has got everything and it can do everything!

You drive off. On the way you want to open the window on one side, so you immediately call the manufacturer. "Could you open the window for me, please? - If you want to and if you can!"
You do the same with the air conditioner. Call the producer, ask him to switch it on for you, if he can or wants to.
What garbage – no one would do that. That is why these technical things are in the car and described in the user guide: to be used.

Exaaaactly!!! No one would think that I told the manufacturer what to do, just because I am using his technical works. That is why he let them being produced and installed.

Fact

It is exactly the same with the Word of God. It is like a user guide for the creature "human" and we find exact instructions what to do or not to do and how to handle it best.
When God says: Jesus has carried your sins to the cross and he died for you, then you can and you should believe that. Just because you take it for yourself, it does not mean you are telling God what to do but you take him up on his offer and you should be thankful for that your whole lifetime. Logical, isn't it?
The Bible describes a lot of facts God has created for us, so we are entitled to take them.

When Jesus says: "I will not leave you, nor forsake you" and "I will be with you until the end of the world", that is a **fact**. It is absolutely illogical and a sign that I question HIM, actually don't believe HIM, if I then pray: "Lord, do not leave me."

Hello...? - what did he just say? I will not leave you! And you say: Lord – please do not leave me – please!
This is blatant and illogical. But unfortunately it is practiced that way by many Christians and unconsciously a wrong picture of Jesus is drawn.

I do know what I am writing about because in my earlier days I was thought like that too, until Jesus showed me it was different. That has changed a lot.

I can only thank Jesus for this statement, clinging to it also in difficult situations. "Thank You, Jesus! Thanks – for Your promise to never leave me."
This is faith the way God likes it.

When God says: Through Jesus' stripes, you are healed, this is a **fact**.

It is a finished act in the past. Done. Finito. Installed (like with the car) and available. Use without questioning the producer. Basta.

Given authority: **fact!**
Proxy: **fact!**
Defeated devil: **fact!**
Called for HIS Kingdom: **fact!**
Signs and wonders following: **fact!**
And much more: **fact!**

This is my experience, my life with Jesus and my way in faith. I do not understand everything and I do not have an answer for each question, but I don't have to. Day by day I learn, seeing the things of faith becoming more developed and established in my life.

I started to write my personal chapter 29 and I can enthusiastically tell you: I am not finished yet – the most amazing things are yet to come because Jesus promised me: I quote once again:

I (Jesus) tell you the truth,
anyone who believes in me (and I do)
will do the same works I have done, and even greater works,
because I am going to be with the Father.
(what an exciting future for me)
John 14:12

Yes! Be carried away on this journey of faith – full of adventures!!

Do you know Jesus?

No way!

You have read this book till here and maybe you think: No way! Never before have I heard or seen anything like this. I only know God or Jesus from religious education in school (we have that in Germany) and I remember it as boring. My grandma once told me something about it but that was not very exciting either. This Jesus and the whole faith thing is something for wimps and weak ones.

Let me tell you, you are terribly wrong there! Jesus, the son of God, is alive and HE loves you, reaching out his hand for you. He wants to save you and to forgive your sin. The sin is not primarily the things you have done or not, it is the sin of not believing in the Name of Jesus. That is the thing standing in between you and God, blocking you from entering into heaven one day.

It is like an injured person who cannot help themselves anymore. There is not self-salvation. So it's no use for the injured one to know that there is an emergency doctor – they must call him! They must entrust themselves to him.

It is not enough to have heard about Jesus and then HE will probably do everything. Jesus is waiting for your invitation, so HE can save you. Everything necessary has already been prepared.
Maybe no one has ever told you that. Maybe you are disappointed with your church or people.

This can change. Invite Jesus to come into your life and to be your Lord, so that you get to know HIM. You will see, Jesus is way different than you might have been told. Sorry – for all the wrong information of others.

A life without Jesus is boring, useless, without future, this is something for wimps. People without Jesus have no idea, what freedom, peace, joy, enthusiasm, power and excitement life can have here on this earth. And furthermore, a life for eternity with Jesus.

Where do You want to spend eternity? What, if they really have a point there with "life after death"? You should have an answer for these existential questions of life. We care about every possible thing in our daily lives. But a lot of people miss caring about eternity with the One whose job it is. Jesus!

Jesus is God's response to our being lost. And sooner or later you cannot get away from this decision. By the time you stand in front of him it will be too late.

Decide now to live with Jesus and to give your life to him. Do not wait for a later or better point in time. There is none. What counts is the now because really suddenly it can be too late.

I invite you, to experience a new life with Jesus, his love, power and forgiveness and to allow HIM to handle Your needs and diseases.
Trust in HIM!

Maybe you are asking, how do I do that?

Just talk to Jesus right now!
You do not have to change beforehand or get better or anything like that.
Talk to HIM, just in the condition and situation you are in right now.
Invite him, receive Jesus. Believe it and then confess it.

The Bible says:

> *But to all who believed him (Jesus)*
> *and accepted him, he gave the right (power, authority)*
> *to become children of God.*
> John 1:12

> *For it is by believing in your heart*
> *that you are made right with God,*
> *and it is by confessing with your mouth*
> *that you are saved.*
> Romans 10:10

It is not difficult. But no one can make this decision for you. Not your parents, not the grandma who has been praying for you for a long time now, no church at all, whatever it's called or whatever it's promised you. Only you and Jesus. Only you can make it right between the two of you, if you receive what he has done.

Jesus will never force you but you should think about it because things can change very fast.
That is why I will write about another thing in this book as well.

After you have just finished reading this sentence, pray to Jesus and lay your life down into the hand of the mightiest, most wonderful, most lovely and most graceful Lord the world has ever known and will ever know.

Jesus Christ

Prayer of salvation

If you want to get to know Jesus and you know that you need forgiveness and salvation, I invite you to pray the following prayer loudly, seriously and full of trust:

Lord Jesus Christ,
I believe and I confess that You are the son of God
and that You came to earth to save me.
You died on the cross for me
and You took my every sin,
for me to be free.
You have risen and You are alive.
I confess my sins to You
and I pray that You would clean me.
I receive You in my life,
YOU are my savior and Lord!

Holy Spirit,
please fill me with the power of God,
so I grow in faith
and see more and more of Jesus.

Amen.

The way forward now

Congratulations! Now you are a child of God! Welcome in the family of God!
You have chosen a new path with Jesus by your side. The Bible describes it as being "born again". It has absolutely nothing to do with reincarnation. You will not come to earth as a different kind of living creature once again. You are a new creature in the Spirit of God. Not externally, but in the spiritual world something marvellous has happened.

> *This means that anyone who belongs to Christ*
> *has become a new person.*
> *The old life is gone;*
> *a new life has begun!*
> 2. Corinthians 5:17

Now your new life in Christ should grow and get strong.

Just like a new-born baby needs care, protection and support in learning, you also need it in faith. You need people who know Jesus and who follow him. Who can show and explain to you, how to live and talk to Jesus. By the way, you call that praying. Not only prayers that have already been phrased by others, but just freely, what is on your heart.

Read the Bible, it's best is to start with the New Testament because that is where Jesus is described and what HE has done and said. You can trust in HIM and in his Word. You will see, it will be more exciting than you might expect it to be now.

You need a living church or parish where you feel at home. A church with people who love Jesus and who are enthusiastic about HIM, telling everyone what HE has just done in their lives. Where the Holy Spirit is allowed to do miracles. Where you and others are prayed for, where healing, liberation and restoration are just normal. Where you can get involved with your talents and gifts and where you can grow. There are more churches than you think.

Do you know, that your life is now in the hand and the care of Jesus? Now he has got permission to put things right in your life and to help You.

You will see!

And everything changed all at once

To come within an inch of death

Report

Earlier on, I told you that situations can change faster than you think. It was in the chapter about the decision for Jesus. And it was meant seriously.

Ok – here is my story.

Saturday, 15th February 2014 – seemed to be just a normal day

After a cosy breakfast with my wife I got ready to go to work for my afternoon shift, as a policeman. I put my uniform on, checked my equipment, looked up the appointment book to see what was happening in the evening after work.

I saw that at 7.00 p.m. we would have a meeting with the youth of our church to talk about Jesus, God, the world and their interests.
They were always very keen and excited to listen to what we have already experienced with Jesus on our journey and how we managed situations successfully with God's help and his wisdom or just to chat with us two "old ones".

I was looking forward to it.

"Ok, dear! I'm ready. Have a nice afternoon, see you later. I love you!"
A big, obligatory kiss – of course!
I grabbed my bag and off I went to work.

As I arrived in my office, I started to prepare the beginning of the shift for the team. That involved checking the roster, the patrol duty, whether anyone had been excused from work or whether there had been any changes between the workers. These are notifications that may have arrived while we were away the last two days.

Which tasks or instructions had our chief ordered for the weekend shift? There were various of preparations to be made.

12 o'clock shift meeting – countdown

Meanwhile, the guys and ladies in my team arrived, grabbed their things and got ready. It started as usual with a meeting and we talked about all the important things. One round of hot, strong coffee, as usual (I like coffee!).

After that, a small talk about everything and anything under the sun and life, shortly after it I went to my computer to finish my work inside. Of course, that is why I am here.

As I wrote something I notice my right arm fell asleep. Strange, I have never had something like that before. I shook my arm thinking maybe I squeezed the elbow nerve. It didn't get better but worse. I realize how this numb feeling went down the right side of my body, without any pain, without any key signature or warning. Just like that.

I felt my right side not only becoming numb but also weak. I had to consciously not fall off the chair. Ok, this was definitely not normal, and not my normal way of leaving a chair. Suddenly I was hanging onto the chair, just like a sack of potatoes.

All the thoughts in my head spun around.
Heart attack? Stroke? Something different? What do I do now?
I needed a quick, useful decision right now. A hundred thousand things were racing through my head.

I had been trained to make decisions in emergencies and patrol duties, to successfully handle a scene in the best way. Kind of an emergency manager and director of operations.

It was also a useful skill now, concerning me personally. In my head I unreeled the program I had learned, checking what to do and what was the best.

So I called two of my colleagues at work who were near, shortly explained my physical condition for them to have the basic information and asked one of them: "Please stay with me and watch me so I do not fall off the chair. Please observe my condition.".

To the second one I said: "Please call the emergency doctor and the chief at his home and let him know. Apparently, I have to be brought to the emergency unit.".

Meanwhile, a third one became aware of what was going on and I asked him to let my wife know, telling her that I was being taken to hospital and that she should please come too.

Then I put my whole stuff into order again, switched off my computer and then the emergency doctor arrived at the same time as the ambulance.
A short greeting followed as we knew each other from a lot of jobs, a short, intensive check-up and then the doc gets very serious. "Casualty unit as fast as possible, suspicion: stroke"!

Drive into the Black Out

I have often driven in an ambulance, racing with sirens into the next hospital as fast as possible. But never lying there as the patient. It was a quite strange feeling.
If you ask me today whether I was afraid, I can say no with a good conscience. I knew that if anything went wrong, veeeery wrong, it was clear to me that it was a matter of life and death at that very moment.

But I knew 1000 percent: my life is in the hand of God, I am in good hands and HE is in control of everything. However, it might end.
Either I will be well again, or I will go to Jesus and see him face to face. The goal of my life would have been reached.
That was why no fear took place in me.

Actually I did not want to go yet. I still had so many things planned, all my goals and visions for my life had not been fulfilled yet. But at that very moment I knew, it was not in my hands.

Laying on that stretcher, brought through the floors to the check up, I prayed: "Lord Jesus, my life is in Your hands!"

So I had done everything I could at that moment.

And then everything went black at once, I had fainted, it was night. Pitch-black night. Without transition. From one second to another. I have never known anything like that. No falling asleep, no softly waning into dreams, just like someone had put a switch off and bam – gone.

All the following incidents that I am explain, I know from Andra, my wife.
The police went to our home and told her what had happened to me. My colleagues from work had took her to hospital

because they did not want her to drive a car in this extraordinary situation.

Before they drove off, Andra told them: "Wait a minute, first I must call someone." She called a friend from our church who belonged to our leadership.
"Please pray, Günther is in hospital, it seems to be something serious, I do not know any more details yet."

Then they drove off, with Andra in the back of the police car. What would meet her? Was the goodbye kiss after breakfast and before work the last kiss she would get from her husband in her life? It was only about three hours ago.

The friend from church activated a so called "prayer line", that means he called everyone from the leadership team, giving them the information and the call to pray. So it went on through the whole leadership, all the church members and the number of praying people increased.
Here I will shorten the description to not go into detail too much. Andra was with me the whole time, I did not know that at the time. She talked with the doctors, agreed or rejected measures they wanted to take. Thank God we had already talked about things like that before. At that time, she was calm, focused and the peace of God surrounded her. Of course, she was tense but not depressed or hysterical.

The doctors who had made the CT unanimously told her the final diagnosis:

strong cerebral haemorrhage, right in the middle of the brain;
the center of language,
memory, planning capacity,
coordination.

Surgical intervention wasn't possible because you would have to irreparably damage important and quite big parts of the brain.
As a result of that, the haemorrhage would have possibly stopped, but after that I would definitely need an extreme cure and help.

They told her, she should give into the inevitable and that after at least two days I would be dead. Because of its strength the haemorrhage would not stop by itself.
These doctors were honest, direct and they did not cause any false hopes.

But they did not reckon the prayer of people who know God and his nature and who love him. Who had already experienced that the prayer of trust releases miracles so many times.

And the prayers were answered!

The first miracle of God was visible!

Surprising the doctors and the staff, the haemorrhage suddenly stopped. It was unexplainable to them and medically it was impossible. They had not experienced anything like that their whole long, specific career yet. These people, the tough fighters for life, they, who day by day competed against death and most of the time lost, they were completely astounded by God.
One of the nurses said she was an atheist but this thing happening here was still a miracle.

In order not to put too much strain on the body, they put me in coma and cooled the body down. (People who know me, also know that I have always liked it a bit cooler, I have never had any problems with chill).

So I was laying there for about ten days. I had no near-death experience, did not see any light shapes or anything similar. Everything was just black and calm.

I had dreams and perceptions but I do not know when they started. Whether it was during the coma or in the initiated recovery phase some time later.

At any rate, it was more than real, a touch with the invisible world, partly extreme, very extreme. Successful confrontations with spiritual forces and some things more. I have decided not to talk about it.

During the recovery phase the doctors explained that Andra should not get her hopes up, because of the haemorrhage a lot of blood had got out and now there was a big bruise at that place in the brain, squeezing the surrounding tissue. Drainage to divert or siphon the blood was not possible.

Andra also informed the brothers and sisters in church about that, so they went on and on and on with prayer. Meanwhile, our friends, brothers and sisters in Germany, Europe, South America, USA and India were praying for us. The pieces of information and the request for prayer had reached them. The internet seems to be good for something.

And the second miracle happened!

I woke up, still pretty dizzy and falling asleep at times, but my language was completely there, my foreign languages, my complete memory, my identity and planning capacity and so on.

You can imagine which cheering and thanks went on with our friends. For Andra and for me. Taken away from death by my beloved Lord Jesus Christ.

During her time of prayer and waiting, Andra had been given a picture by God in her spirit. She had seen God's mighty hand over my head and from that very moment she knew: God will take care of it and Günther is secure in his heavenly father! That made her be calm and despite the strenuous, tumultuous time she had the peace of God in her heart.

Nevertheless, there was a problem.

I was paralyzed on the right half of my body.

The arm was totally weak and useless, I could not stand and either lay in bed or sat in a wheelchair. All my muscles in the right half of the body were paralyzed. There was a numb sensation as if I had got an anaesthesia injection which was now losing its effect. But that's not all. The brain had cancelled the nerve pathways and deleted them from the program.

Hurrah, right? Not a very good scenario, but I was alive! And therefore I was so eternally grateful to God.

I had been so close to death, about to finish my life here abruptly and to be with Jesus for eternity. I had not been afraid, I had and still have the absolute certainty that I am saved and that I am going to live with Jesus for eternity.
God is the Lord over life and death and my time is in his hands. And I do look forward to be with him one day.

Do not give up

But I like to live, too! And honestly, I had not really finished with it yet.
During my rehabilitation, a psychologist came to me and we talked about everything. Among other things, she asked me whether I had ever had or still had thoughts about suicide. (Later I was told that this was not that rare among people in such a situation because they did not have a good outlook for their lives.)

Well, what are they talking about! On the contrary! Me and suicide! It's enough to make a cat laugh!

I was and am highly motivated and happy about life! God had offered me some more time here to use. The last few years HE had shown me / us what HE still wanted to do with us. And by that point in time we had just started to discover and walk in these ways.

But between this departure and my situation, first, there was a wheelchair.

Once again, I was in a condition where I had to master a tricky situation and to victoriously manage it.
I had to start to overcome.

Overnight almost everything changed. The things that seemed to be important before, suddenly were not anymore. The things we'd planned for the whole year had to be cancelled.
One week later we would have been going skiing and were to have a healing conference in Austria, as well. In April/May our missionary trip to Argentina and Brazil was planned, like every year. The flights, hotels, hire cars, were already booked and payed for. The church services with the churches there were terminated and so on.
Everything cancelled!

Each day I thanked Jesus for my life and concentrated on my rehabilitation. Here I would like to give great thanks to all the professional help and the huge kindness I have experienced. God bless you for that.

And the miracles went on. From the early rehab I was allowed to join a service in our church, only for a few hours but better than nothing. A married couple, who are pastors in Austria, were in our church for a visit, so I could be there for one of the meetings.
Welcome back to spiritual life.

Like!

They prayed for me and what had just been impossible, was possible at once. The upper thumb member of my right hand was moving, namely with intention. I could control it although the doctor had said the nerves were not active. I cried because of joy because I also saw it as a pointer of God, that HE had started to bring me forward.

Thumbs up! I like it!
God has got a fantastic humor, of all of them to start with the thumb.

Back to rehabilitation. The next day the therapist came and asked how my weekend had been. Without a word I held my thumb up to her and moved it.
It took a moment, then she cried out. "Impossible, it is incredible, no way, the thumb just cannot move!". She jumped off her chair, ran through the whole station, rounding up nurses, other therapists and everyone she could find.

As if in a circus I had to show this little movement again and again, moving the thumb member, moving, moving, moving. They applauded, showed their amazement and partial bewilderment, and asked how this could have happened.

It was a great opportunity for me to talk about Jesus with them again and again.

I knew that I had to start doing the things I could again and which God had given me to do. Preaching and praying for people.

And Jesus was by my side.

Sitting in the wheelchair, I laid my healthy hand upon the sick and they became healthy. People were touched and changed by the preaching. Wow – who would have thought that.

Again, in my head there were these battles of thoughts.
"You are out of your head! Look at yourself, you are a cripple and you want to pray for others?"

And it went on like this. Step by step I recaptured my spiritual service. Go on, do not give up.

Rehabilitation is still is intensive today and without question strenuous. Sometimes I come home, fall into my bed completely exhausted and I sleep for a few hours like a log

I am still pretty disabled, I can't resume my job as a policeman yet, but one day I will be fit again and will maybe go back to work, eat independently, have a shower and do all the other things in life. Right now, time, patience and endurance are necessary.

God will help me, that is as sure as anything.

> *And I am convinced that nothing can*
> *ever separate us (**ME**) from God's love.*
> *Neither death nor life,*
> *neither angels nor rulers,*
> *neither our fears for today nor our worries about tomorrow -*
> *not even the powers of hell*
> *can separate us (**ME**) from God's love.*
> *No power in the sky above or in the earth below – indeed,*
> *nothing in all creation will ever be able*
> *to separate us (**ME**) from the love of God*
> *that is revealed in Christ Jesus our (**MY**) Lord.*
> Romans 8:38-39

> *A song for pilgrims ascending to Jerusalem.*
> *"I look up to the mountains -*
> *does my help come from there?*
> *My help comes from the LORD,*
> *who made heaven and earth!*
> Psalm 121:1-2

Life is not a game

Maybe you wonder, why in the world is he telling me that now. Actually it completely contradicts what he has written in this book. Don't get yourself in a twist "God is good" and so on.

But it just belongs to that. I would not be honest if I withheld it. Anyway, it would not make sense. On the contrary, in my opinion it shows that everything is as I have described it. That there is hope, that God steps in and that he is still good, even if I do not understand anything or cannot explain everything yet.

If everything went smoothly in life, no difficulties or problems, no challenges, we could not show what we believe in and what is in us.

For example, there would be no inventions.
Let's think of Edison, the ingenious guy. First, the light appeared inside his head, then this crazy thought evolved into a concrete and a clear vision. But that was when the work just started. Experimenting, testing, digesting setbacks, starting again and everything anew.
He did not give up and allegedly it took more than 1000 attempts until this dim light worked. In 1879, he announced his patent. done – he had overcome the problem and won.

Still today one of his light bulbs is hanging in fire station 6 in the town of Livermore in California, USA, near San Francisco. And since 1901 (!) it has been burning without any interruption. Meanwhile, a live webcam is focused on it to prove this.

Imagine if Edison would have given up after the 999th attempt. I mean, he had the possibility to do that, at this point in time he did not know how close he was to get the invention done.

In many other parts of our lives it is like that. Challenging things happen, put a strain on us, annoy us and we do not know why they are happening.

In the Bible we can find plenty of hints that we will be met by big needs sometimes. At any time, all human beings. How we deal with it makes the only difference.

Martin Luther once gave this heading to Psalm 46:

Our God is a solid fortress!

There is nothing mightier, more safe and more solid than the God of the Bible, the father of our Lord Jesus Christ and the wonderful power of his Holy Spirit. Read it yourself!

God is our refuge and strength,
always ready to help in times of trouble.
So we will not fear when earthquakes come
and the mountains crumble into the sea.
Let the oceans roar and foam.
Let the mountains tremble as the waters surge!
Psalm 46:1-3

So this is also valid for you and me!

I have been a policeman for more than 40 years now and during this time I have often experienced how people deal with trouble. From fleeing into alcohol, drugs, excesses, adrenalin and in the end in suicide. Because they were disoriented people, had no one who could really help them and obviously they had had no one telling them about Jesus. Or they did not want to hear and believe it. What a drama.

God has not changed his calling for my life, he has not revoked it or kept it on ice just because I am disabled at one wing at the moment. Or because my trying to walk looks like one of the "Augsburger Puppenkiste" (it is a popular German marionette theatre).
It does not matter – we go on with Jesus.

Jokingly, I compare it to a car that has had an accident on the right half. Flat tire and a dent in the fender! However, it stays a car with its calling to be a car.

So it will not change – God is good!

To come to a conclusion, I would like to make this clear once again because it is my conviction from the bottom of my heart:

- God is good!
- Jesus loves me infinitely!
- HE does not make me sick!
- It was and is not a lesson from God!
- God only wants my very best!
- I can always trust in HIM!
- My life is HIS forever!

We can entrust our life to HIM, with all its needs and challenges but also the things that please and excite us.
I hope this book could excite and motivate you to set off for new dimensions and experiences with God or to invite Jesus into your life.

Come on and write with me the next chapter of the

Book of Acts 29!

Your personal chapter. It is going to be the chapter that changes our world before Jesus comes again. Millions of people all around the world will come to Jesus, be healed, change their lives and Islam will lose its power because the power of Jesus will be visible again. It cannot stand against Jesus. These days, more Muslims are coming to Jesus than they did in the last 1400 years! Christians will get to know the supernatural power of God as just being normal, they will

appreciate it and use it in this world. They will do signs and wonders and the news will be full of it.
Some churches and parishes will stay in the weakness and dilution of their theology, conviction and non-expectancy but it was already like that when Jesus was around.

But those who step out and follow Jesus will see signs and wonders, lifting up Jesus. They will not be able to understand and explain everything and they will have to go through situations and overcome themselves but they will be victorious.
I wish and I pray that you are among these Christians.

God bless you

Günther Kunstmann

Epilogue:

Again and again we are asked, what about this biblical healing; if you are still allowed to go to the doctor or if the fact that you are sick means you are Christian who is weak in faith.
Does God want to heal even today? Does he want to teach us lessons through a disease or do we glorify him by it?
The controversial positions towards this topic within the Christian area are known to us.

So really briefly I would like to take up these basic points here; they reflect our knowledge and the opinion of our church, the Jesus Gemeinde Bamberg. Others might see it in a different way – well then, it is their responsibility and their right.

Diseases can have various reasons; inherited, self-inflicted or through no fault, biological or mental and so on but they can also be of demonic origin.

God is a God of love and a good father, he basically does not make people sick. It is the foundational will of God that HE wants to heal people, so we can have a blessed and healthy life.

In the New Testament, Jesus is always testified to have healed all the sick who came to HIM or who asked HIM for help. Jesus was without sin and he put the absolute will of God into practice here on this earth.

If God would have made the people sick but Jesus healed them again, HE would have sinned against the father in heaven because HE would have worked against his plans.

I won't go into more theological explanations of this wide-ranging topic, this is another instructive topic and it would go too far now.

So, how do I and we as a church deal with it?

- For us, there is no competition with medicine and doctors and we do not see them as "enemies" or anything like that. They are a God-given possibility to meet diseases and to bring help and relief to the people so they are supported to get well again.

- We cannot agree with so called alternative medicine, such as homeopathy or other methods, because their origins lie in other religions or beliefs.

- The apostle Luke himself was a doctor, and he was also called to follow Jesus.

- If necessary, we also go to a normal doctor as a precaution or for treatment and we do not think this means a person if weak in faith. Special measures or medicine ordered by the doctor should be taken responsibly.

- Of course, we also pray for sick people, trusting and believing in the Word of God because it gives us the instructions as Christians to pray like that (e.g. Mark 16:15-20).

- Because of the biblical example given, we do not only pray for people by laying hands upon them, but we also command the rulers or the disease to bow down before the Name of Jesus and to leave, just like Jesus did and there are many scriptures that tell us to do so because we have been given authority by Jesus.

- This does not only happen in our church but in evangelical, catholic and other free churches, too.

- Healing can appear in several ways:

spontaneous complete healing, an unexpected but visibly beginning process of healing or healing not being visible yet. However, this last one should not discourage us to go on praying for the sick as we know that God touched this person anyway, so we can also pray for clarity about the situation and its background.

- Whether a church member is sick or not, does not indicate his/her level in faith nor influence his/her function or responsibility in the church.

- We encourage people we have prayed for, to go to the doctor and let the healing be confirmed. We never give the advice to just leave off measures or medicine ordered by the doctor because of "faith reasons". That is something only the attending doctor decides.

- Healing prayer is free for all people, just like all other biblical actions.

- All honor and thanks go to Jesus and not to the one who has laid hands upon people to receive healing.